Bella*Blue

Adult Coloring Book

Over 60 full pages!

Pictures Patterns Designs

Danielle Koziol

Open Sky Publications

Drawings, front & back cover design & layout
by: Danielle Koziol

Also by the Author/Artist:

"Dragonflies In July," a novel

"The Chosen Path - A Memoir: True Story
of the 39-Mile Massachusetts Tornado"

www.DanielleKoziol.com
www.DragonfliesInJuly.com

For more artwork/photography,
facebook.com/DanielleKoziol

ISBN: 978-0-9794609-1-3

Color Test Page:

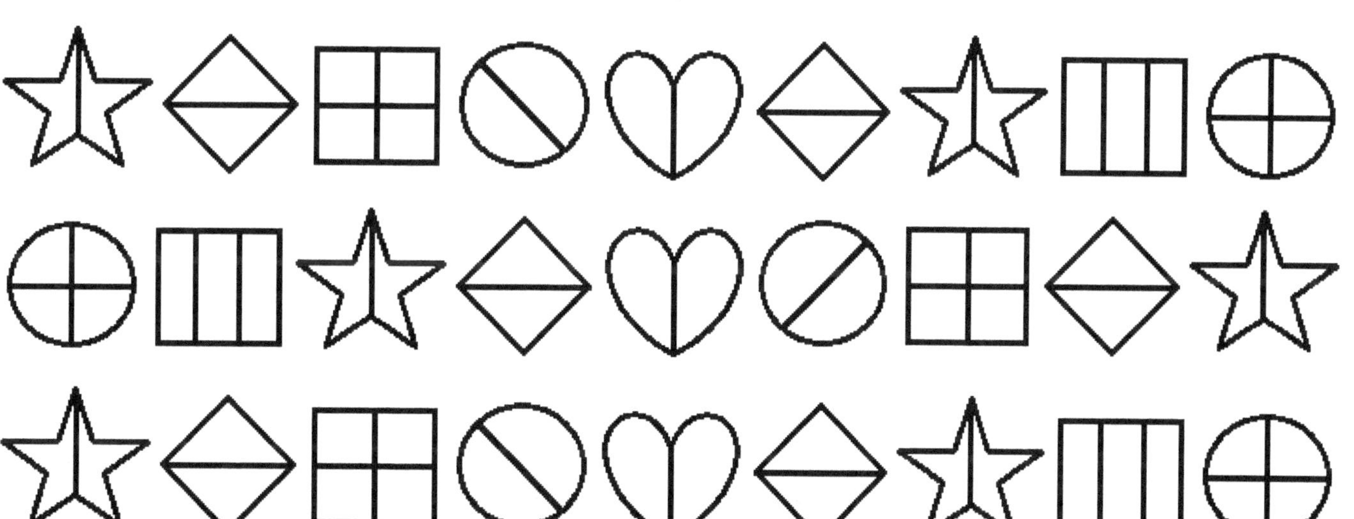

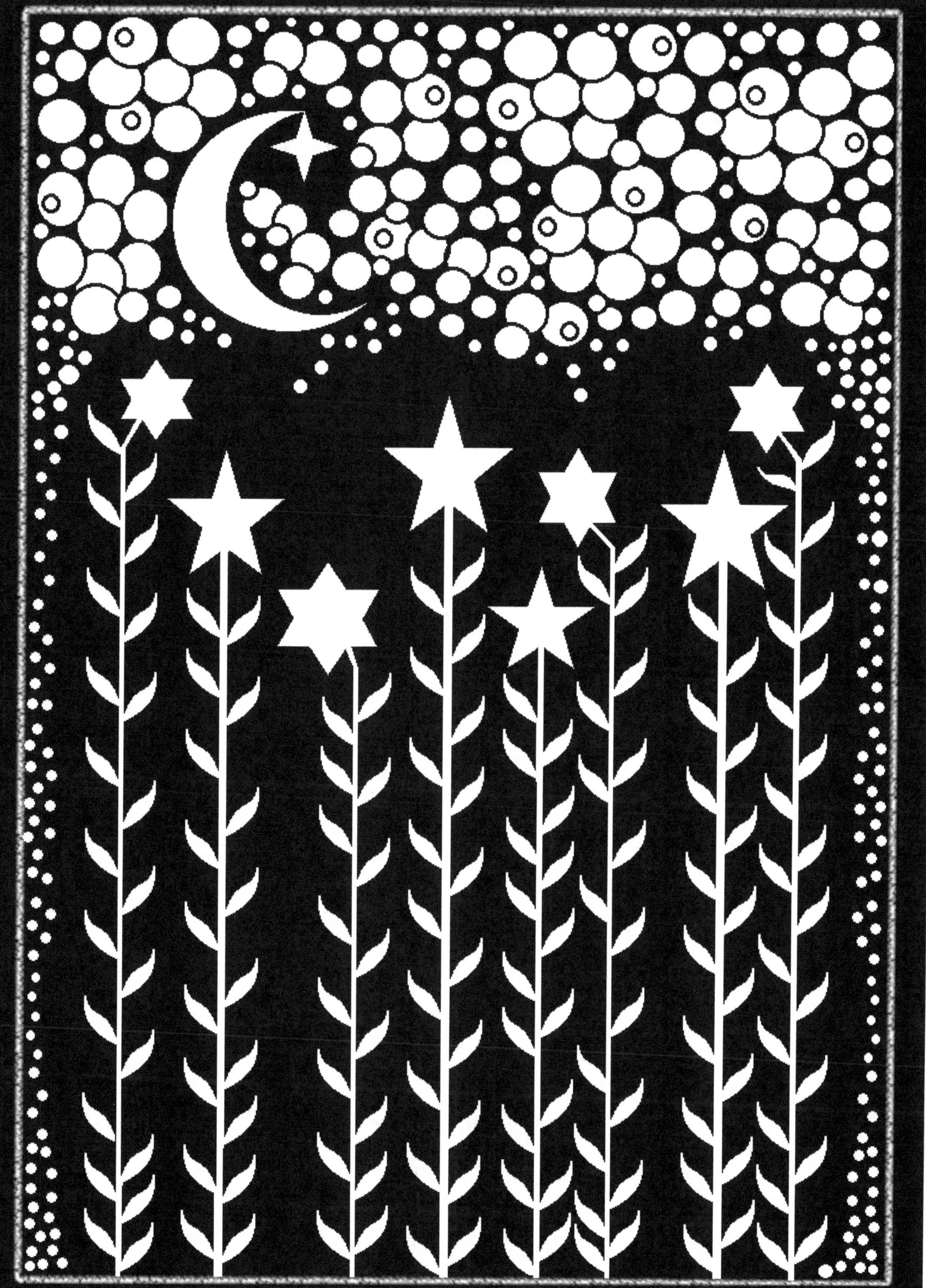

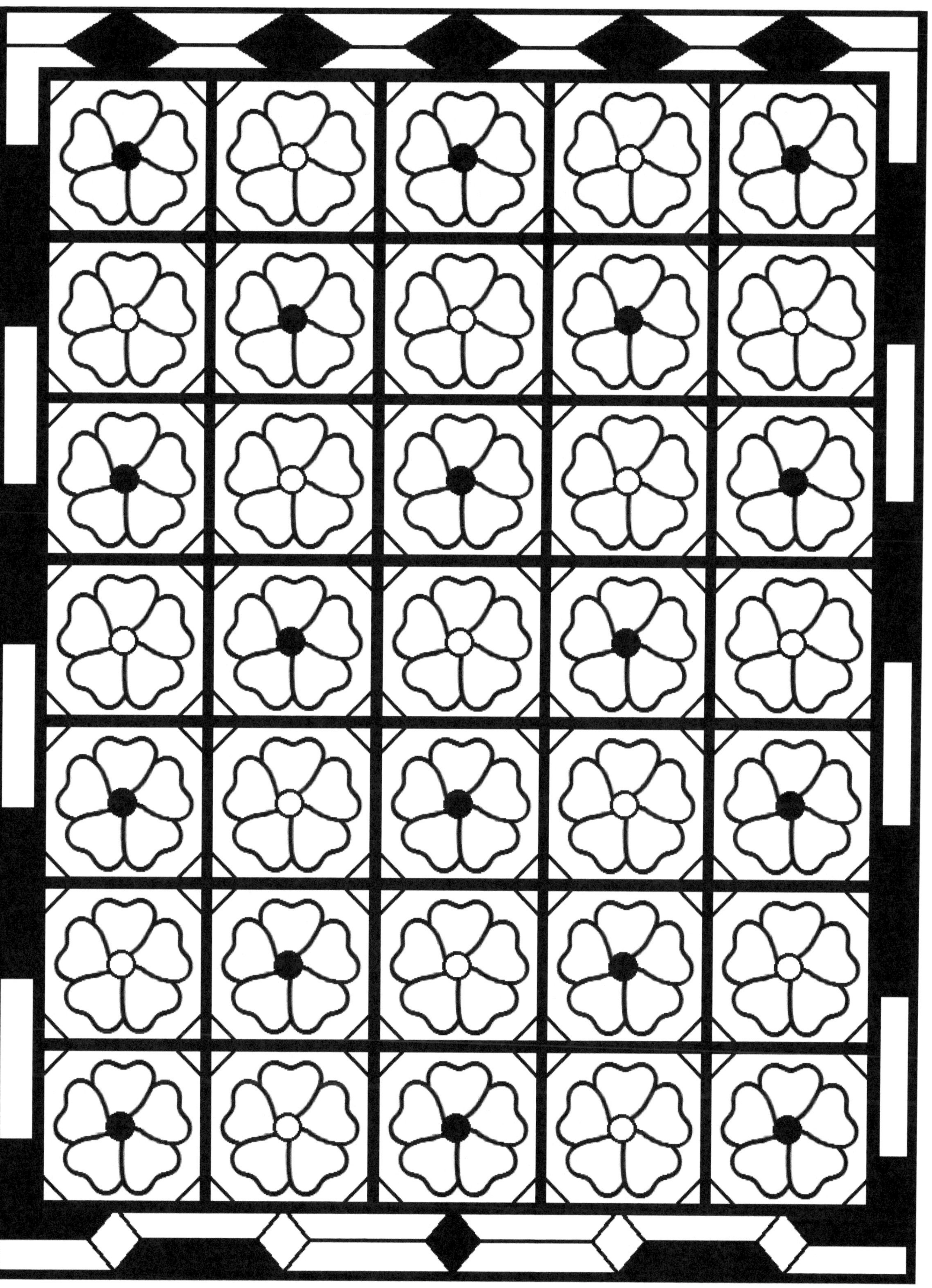

Bella Blue
Adult Coloring Book

find it on Amazon.com

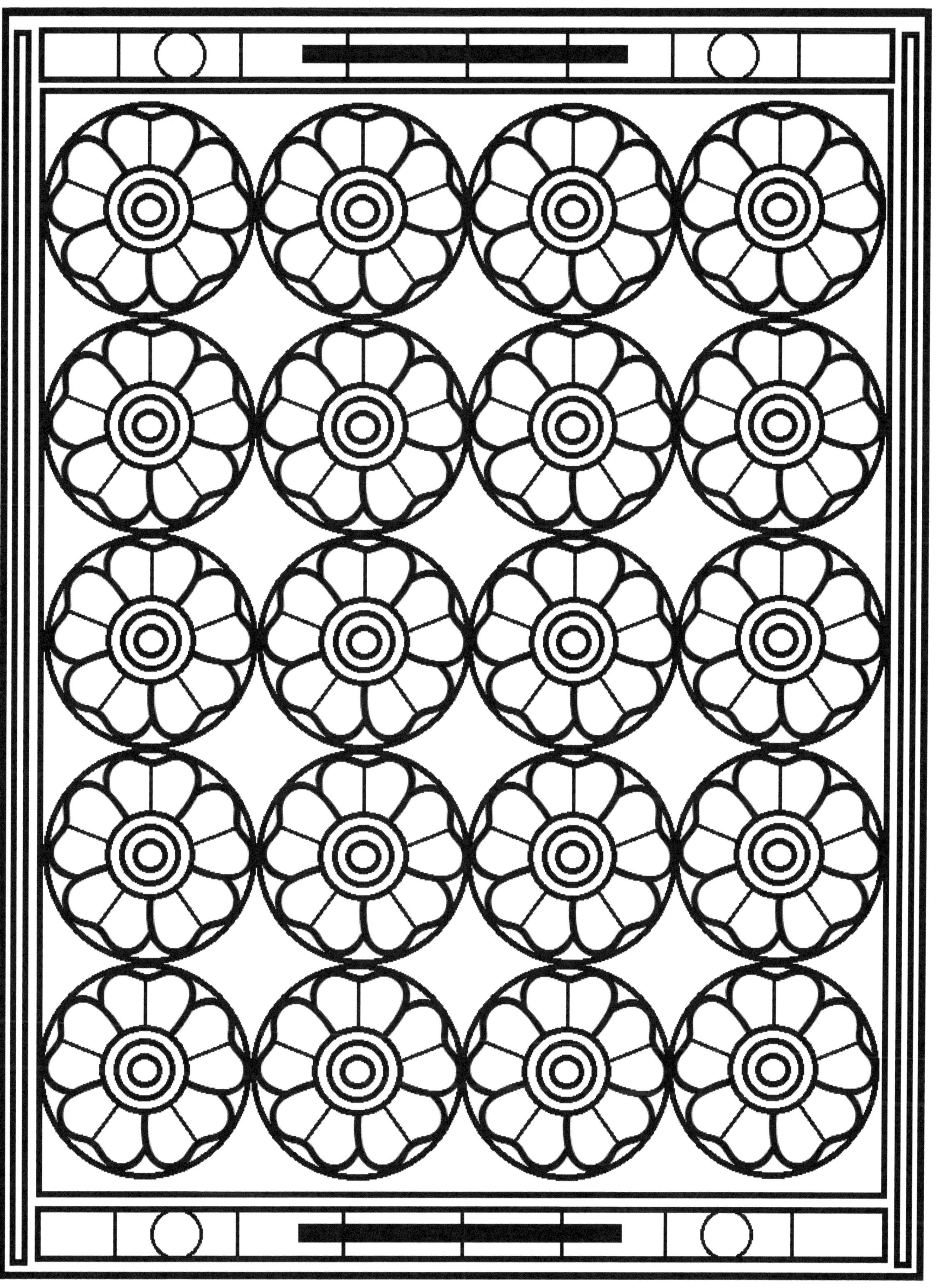

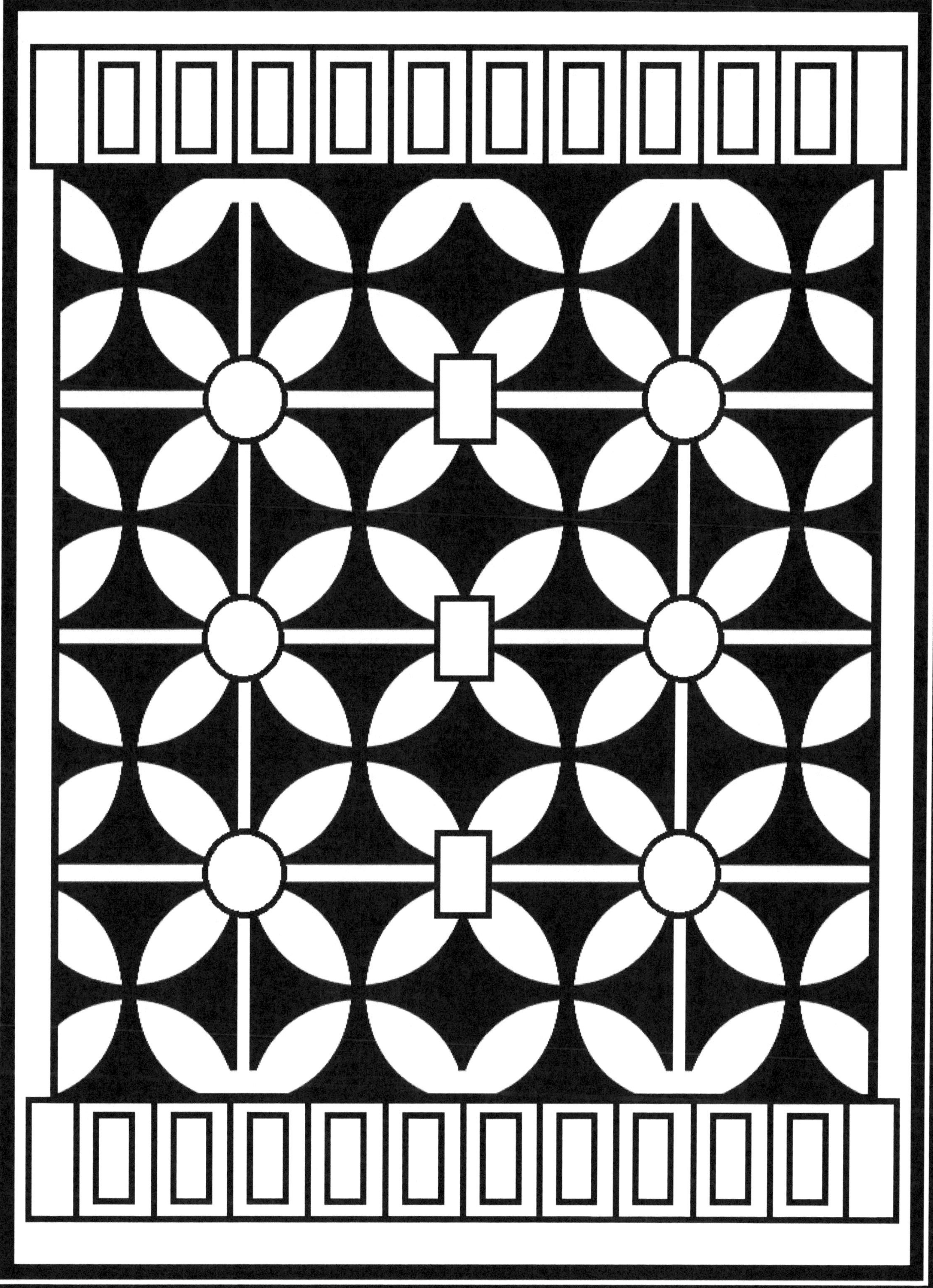

Bella Blue
Adult Coloring Book

find it on Amazon.com

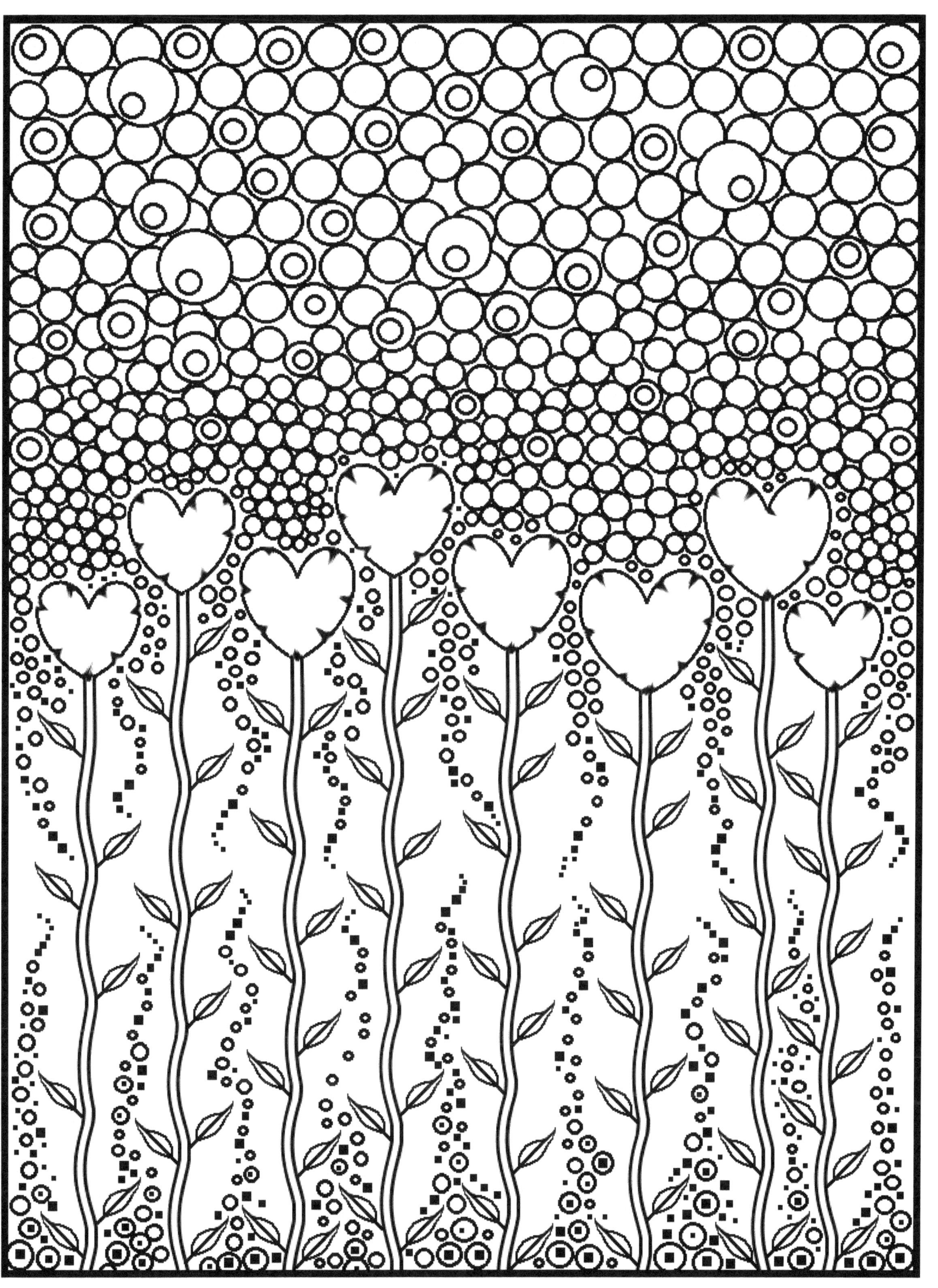

Bella Blue
Adult Coloring Book

find it on Amazon.com

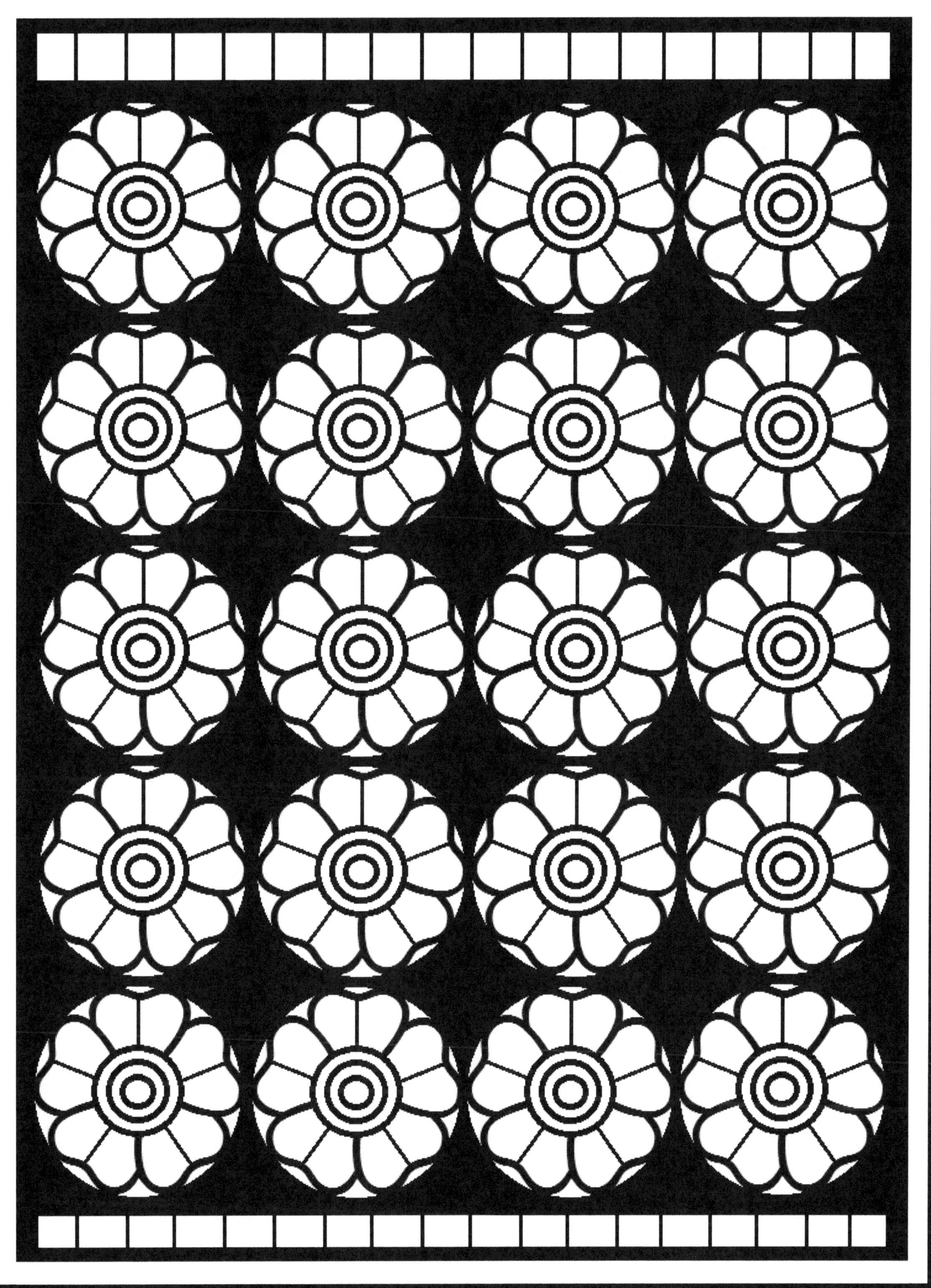

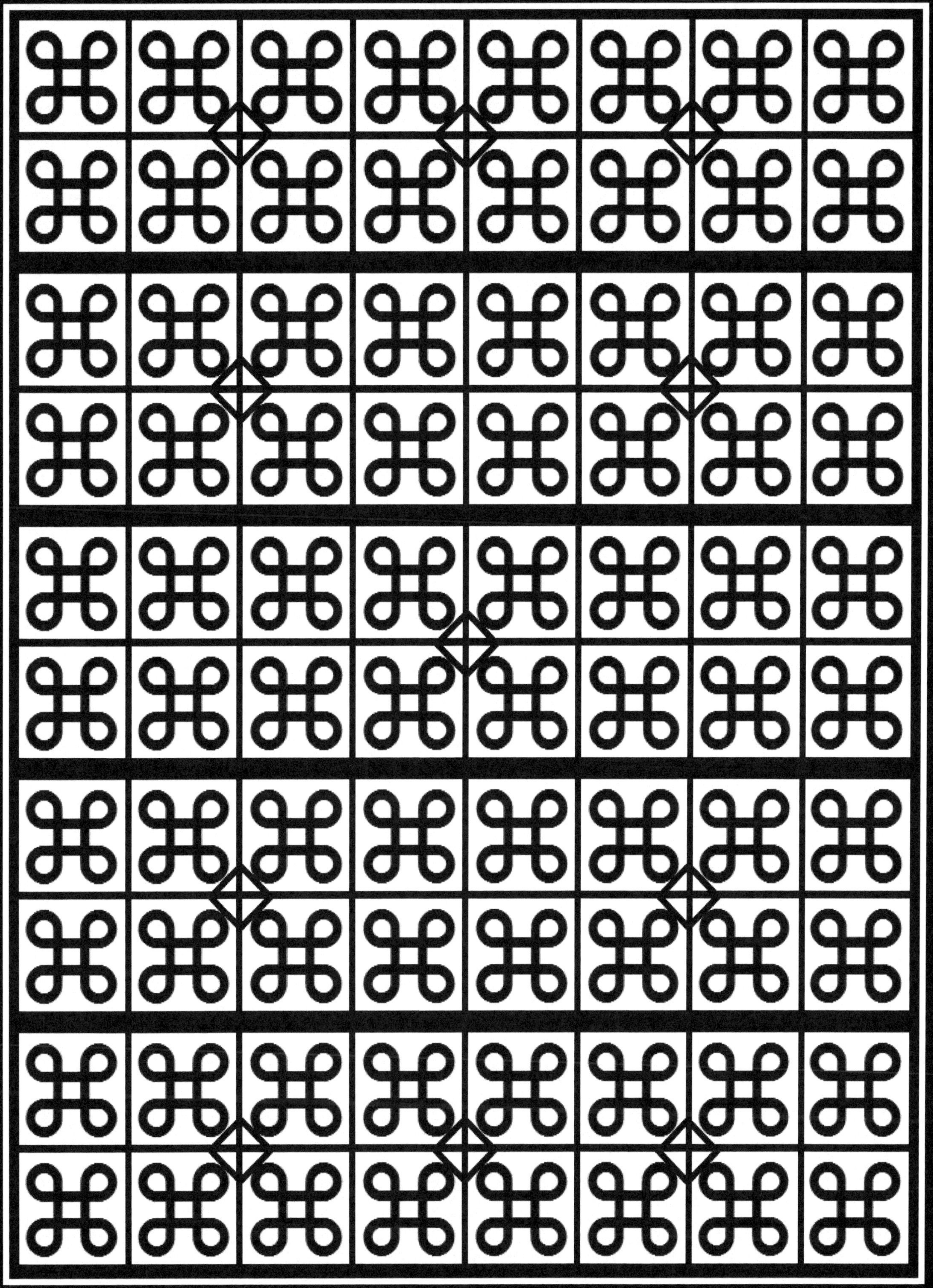

Bella Blue
Adult Coloring Book

find it on Amazon.com

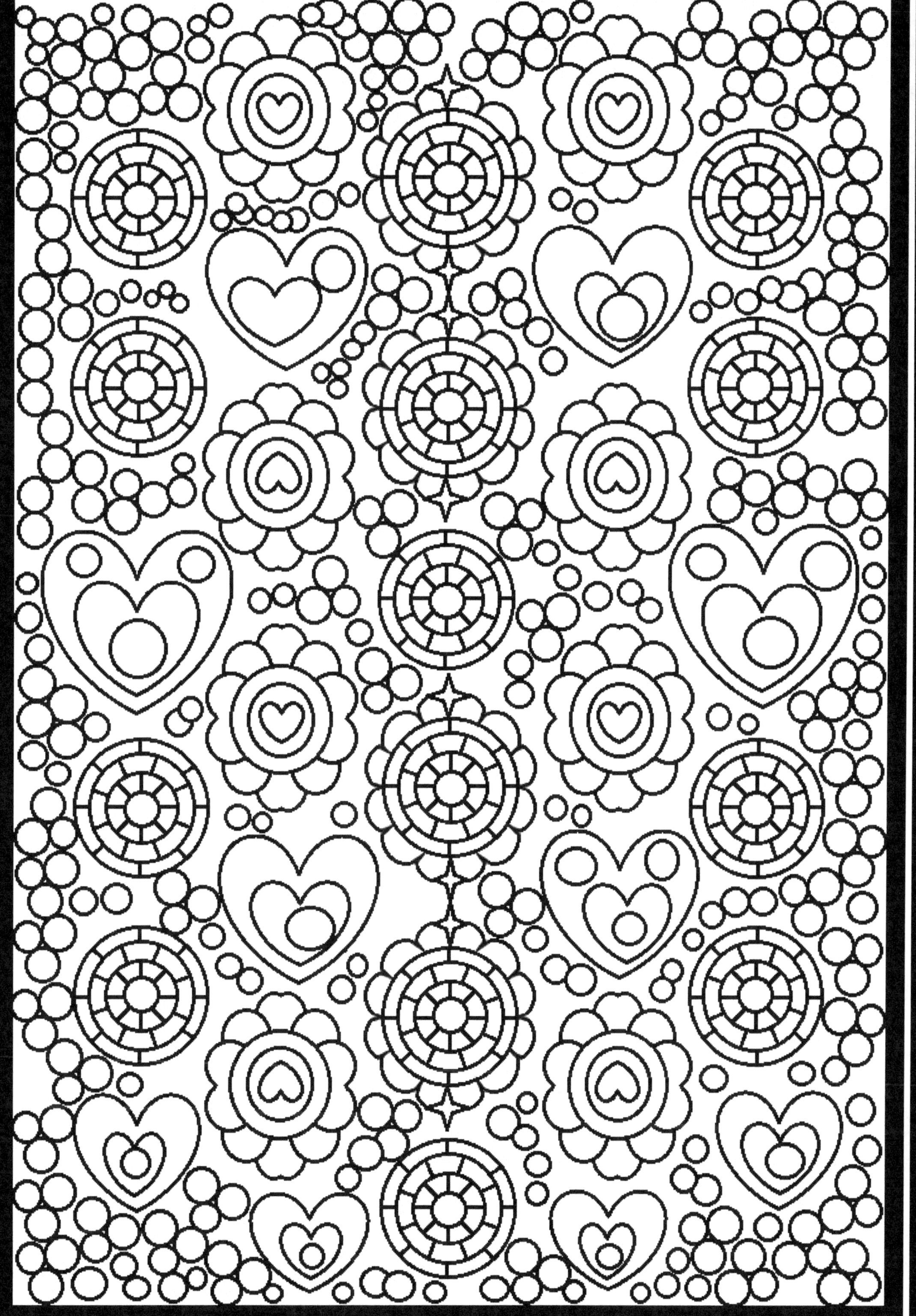

Bella Blue
Adult Coloring Book

find it on Amazon.com

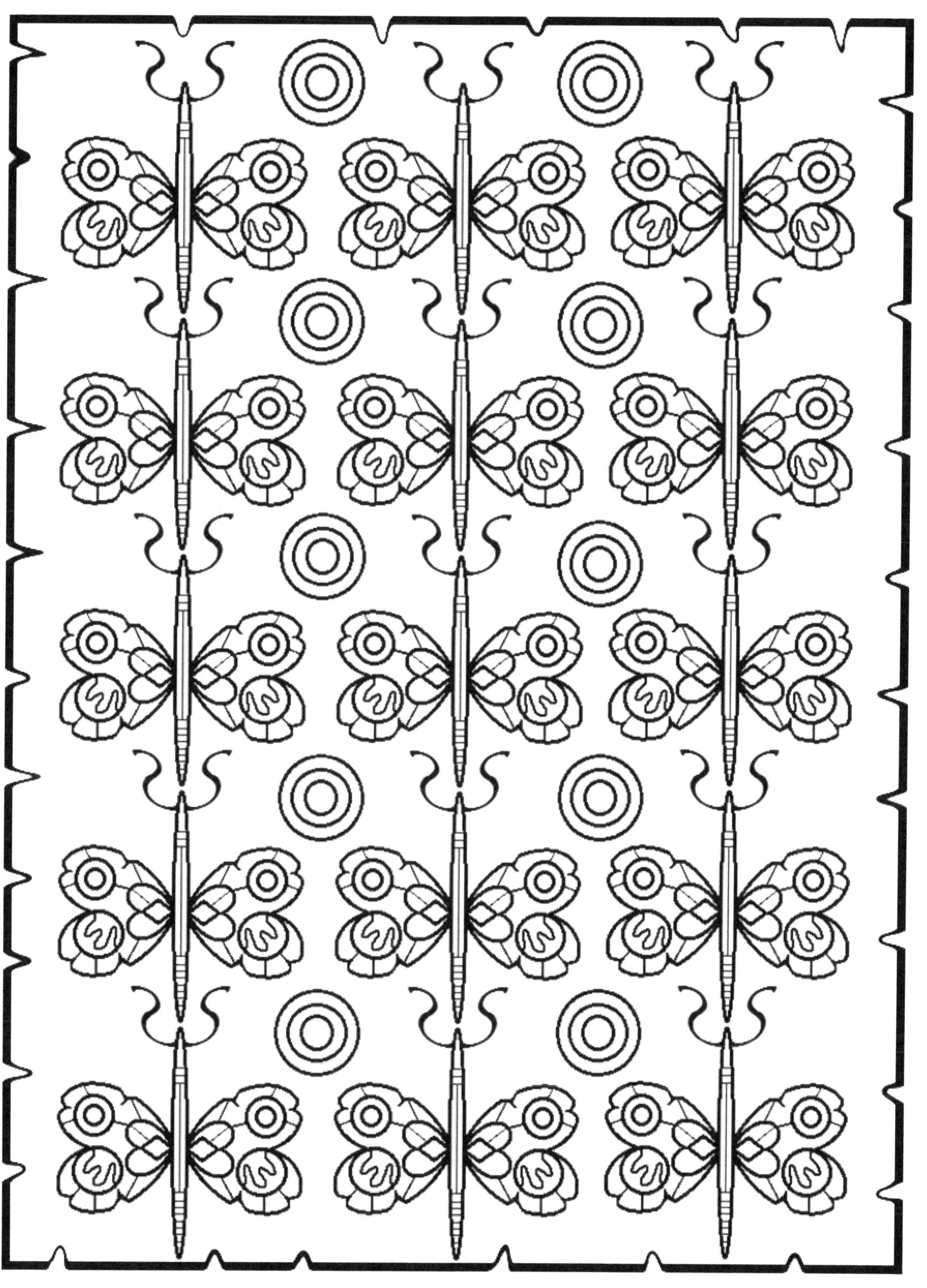

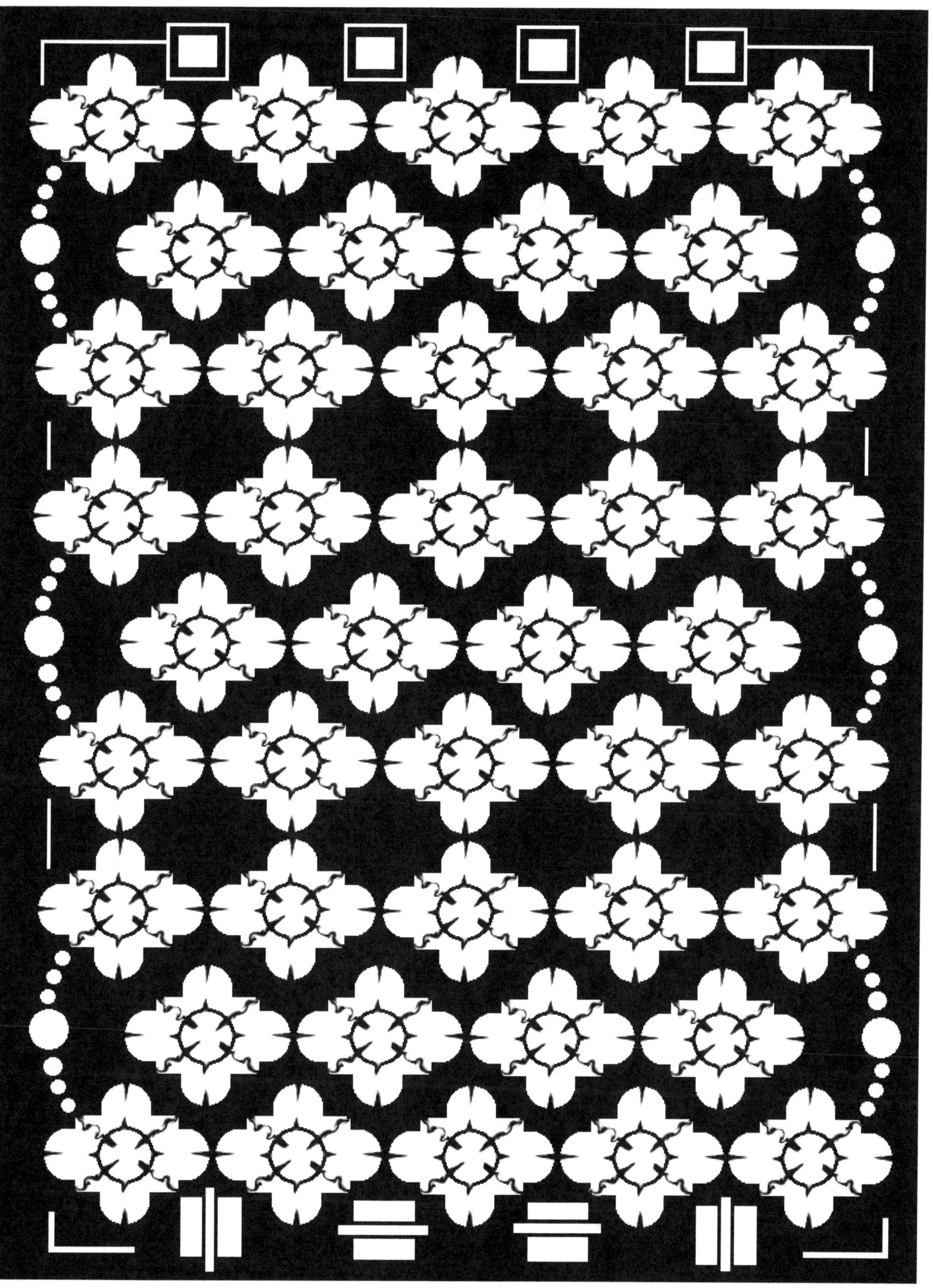

Bella Blue
Adult Coloring Book

find it on Amazon.com

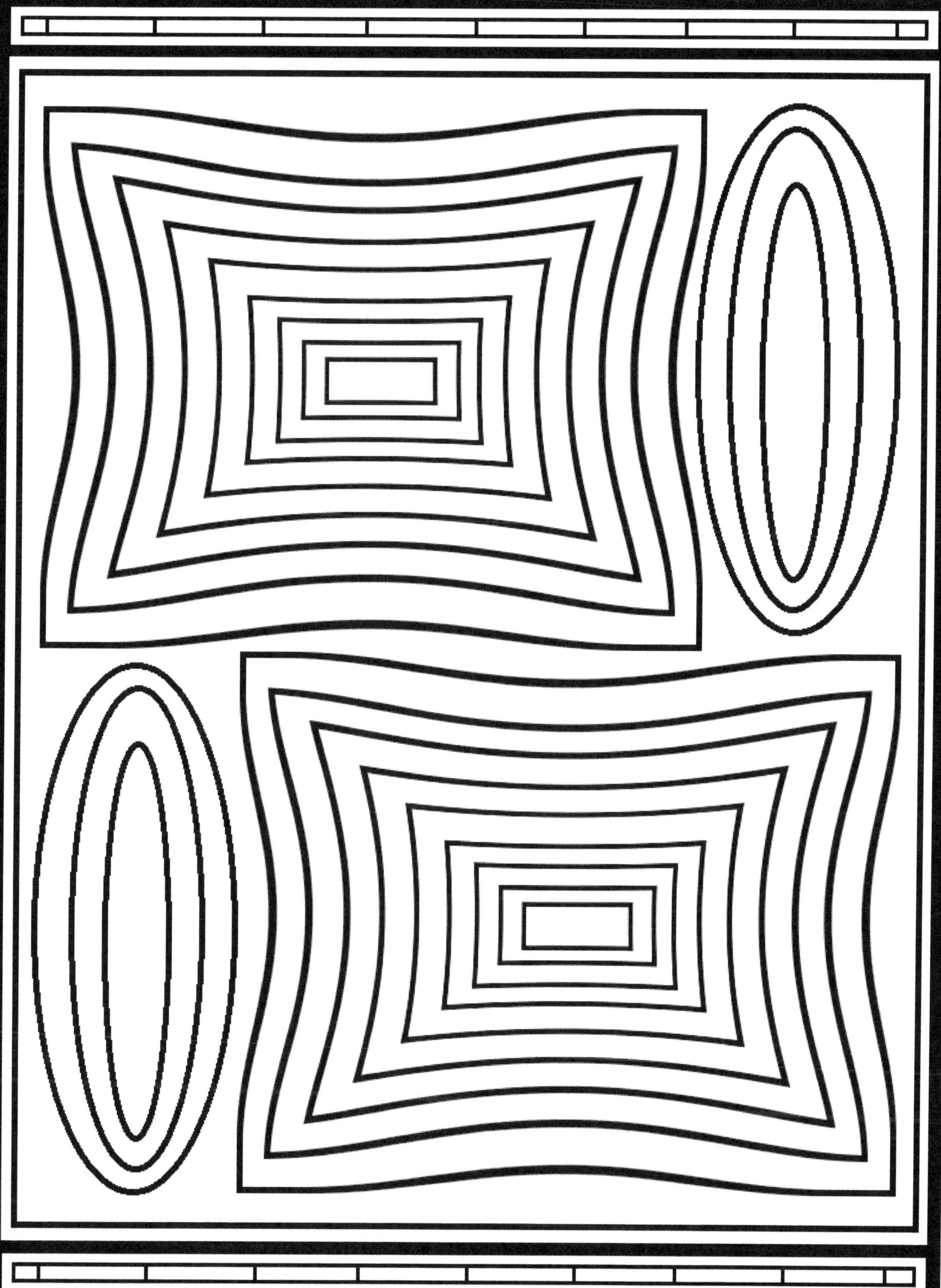

Bella Blue
Adult Coloring Book

find it on Amazon.com

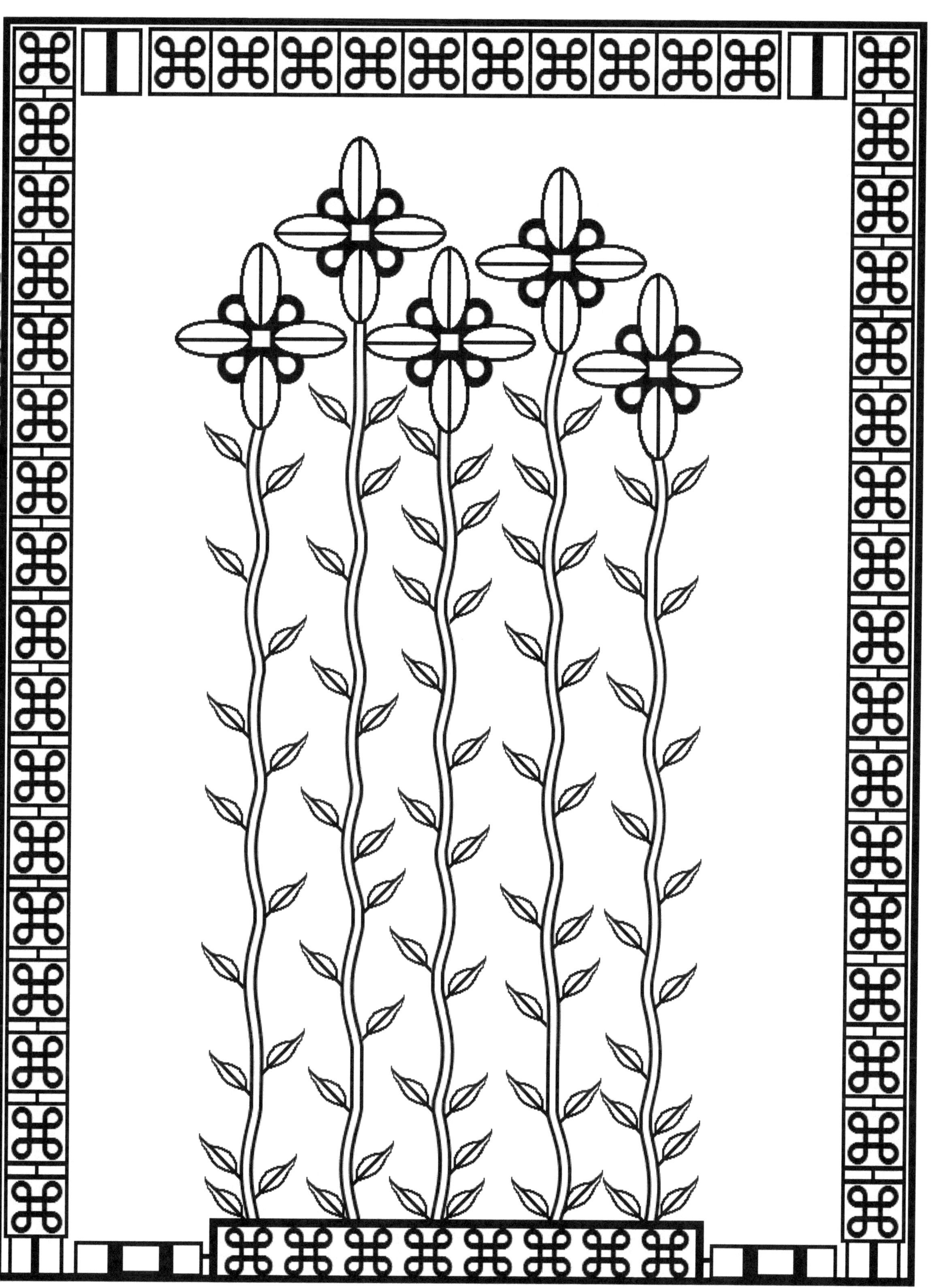

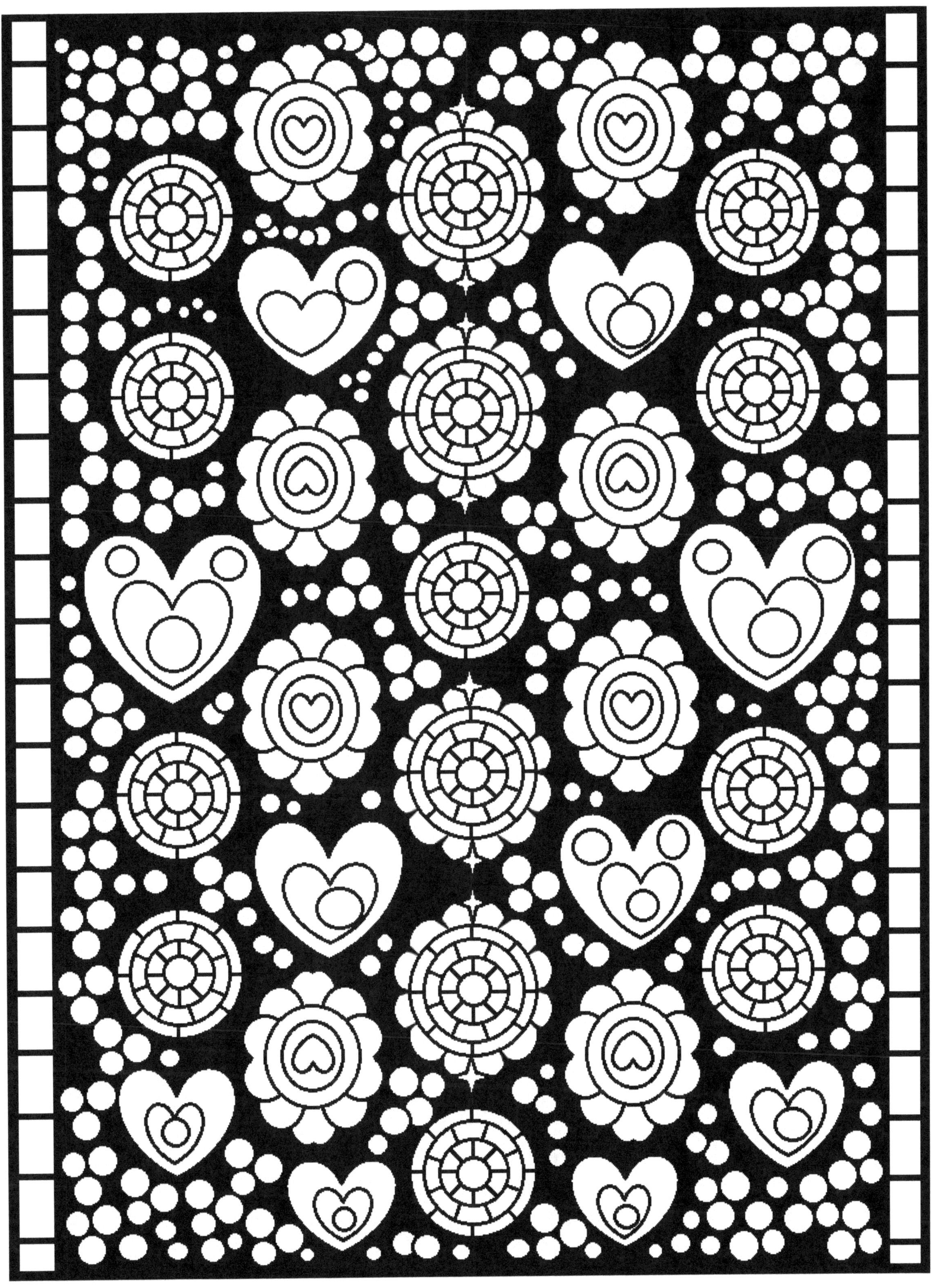

Bella Blue
Adult Coloring Book

find it on Amazon.com

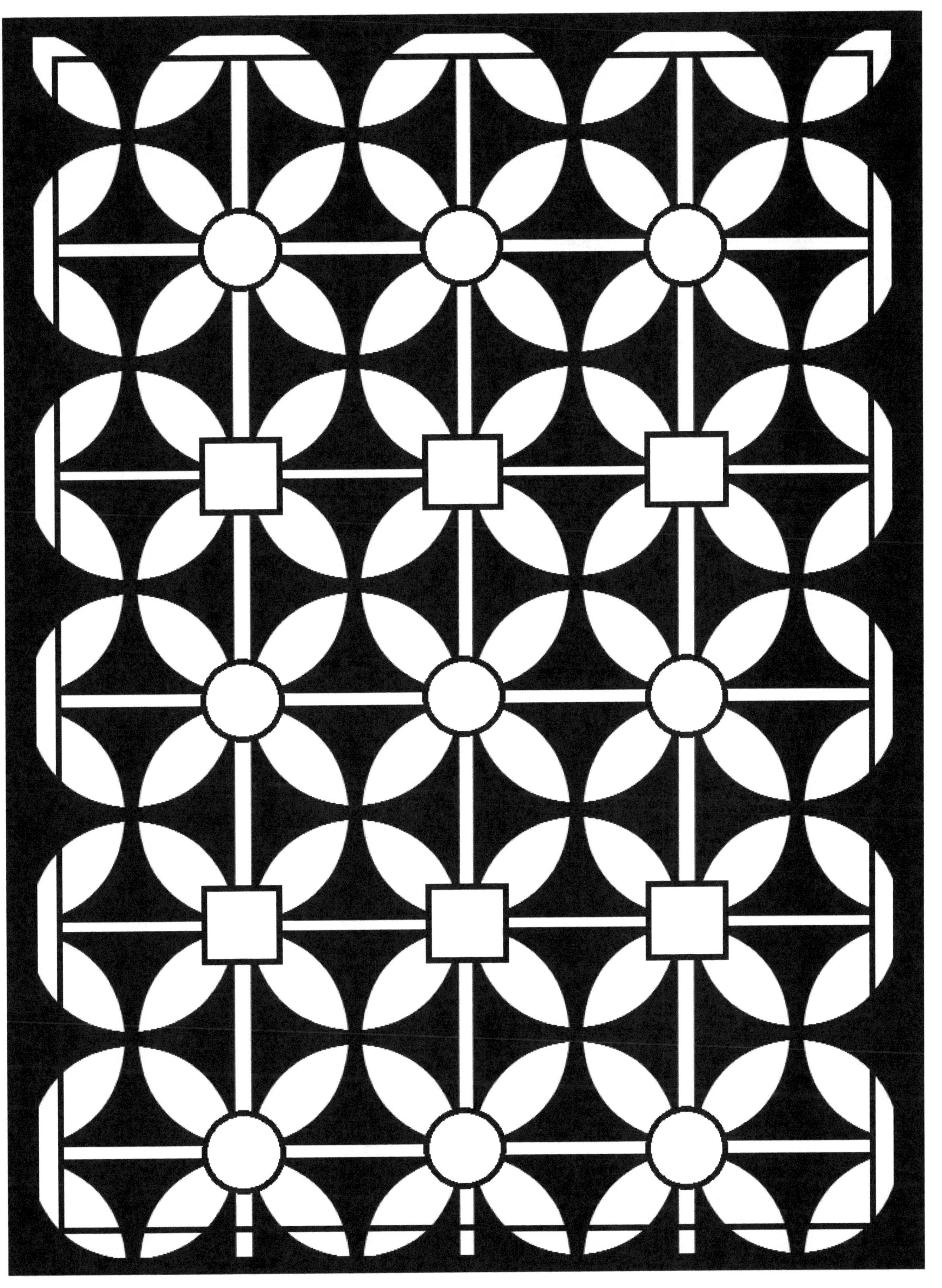

Bella Blue
Adult Coloring Book

find it on Amazon.com

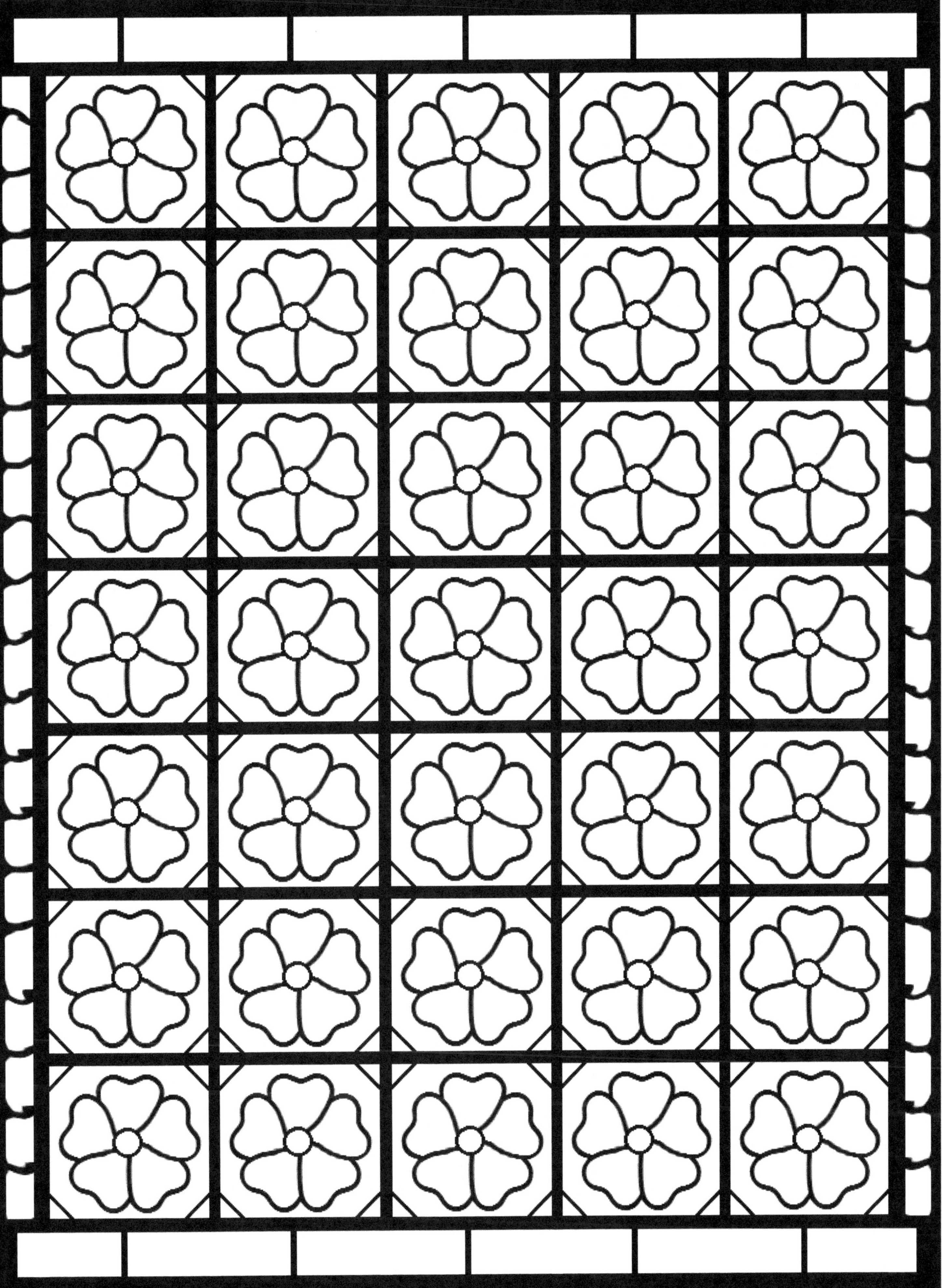

Bella Blue
Adult Coloring Book

find it on Amazon.com

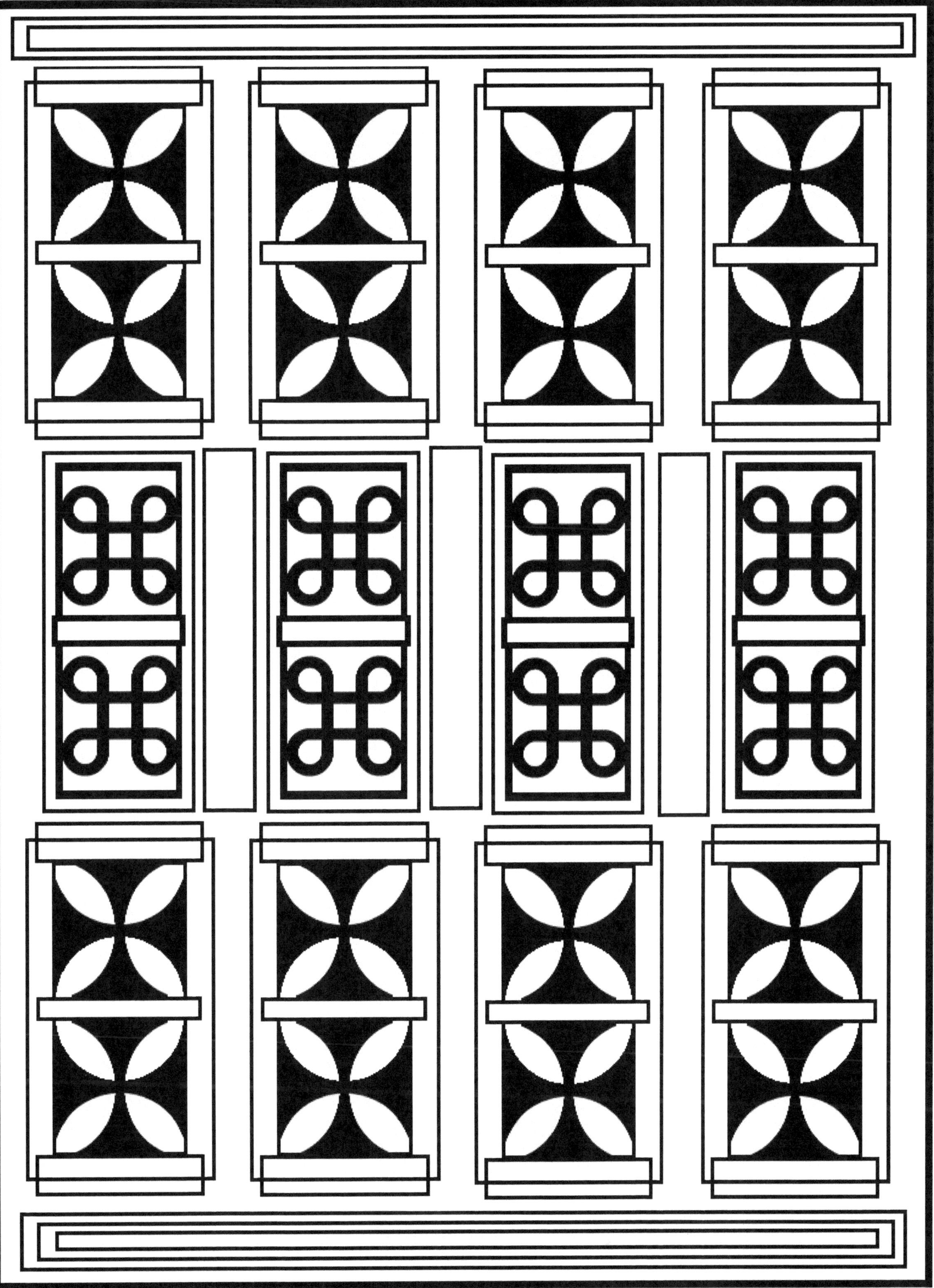

Bella Blue
Adult Coloring Book

find it on Amazon.com

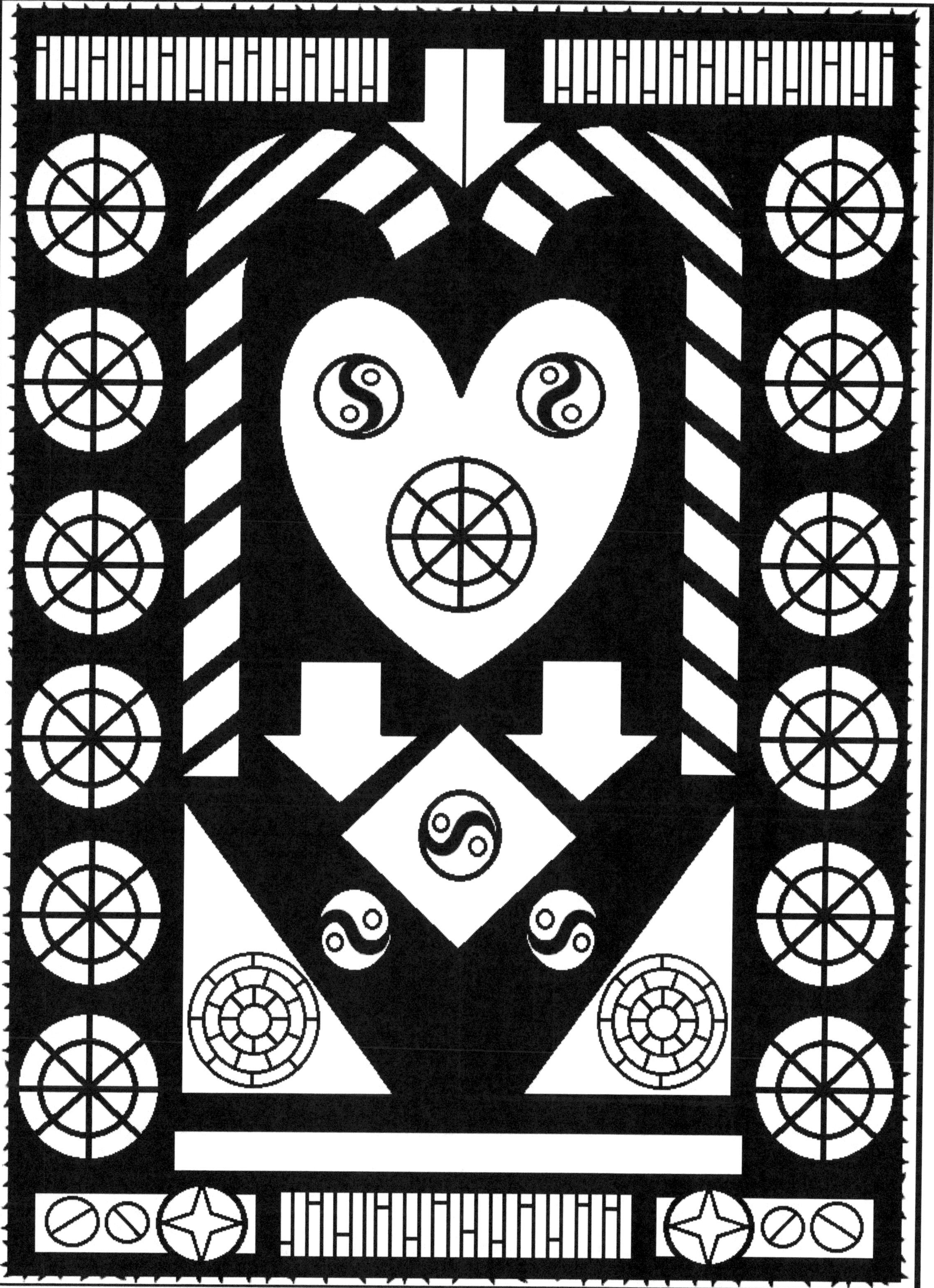

Bella Blue
Adult Coloring Book

find it on Amazon.com

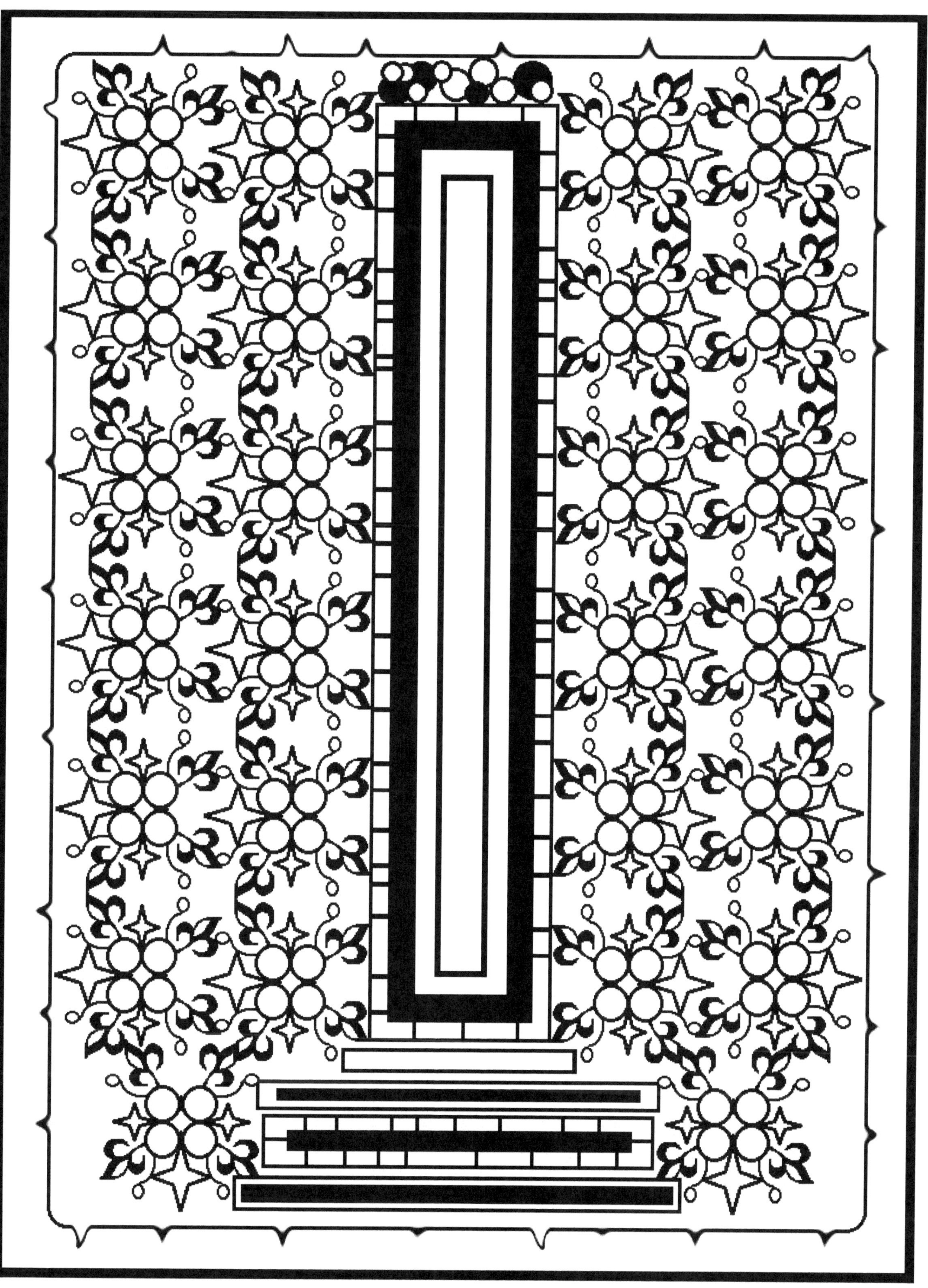

Bella Blue
Adult Coloring Book

find it on Amazon.com

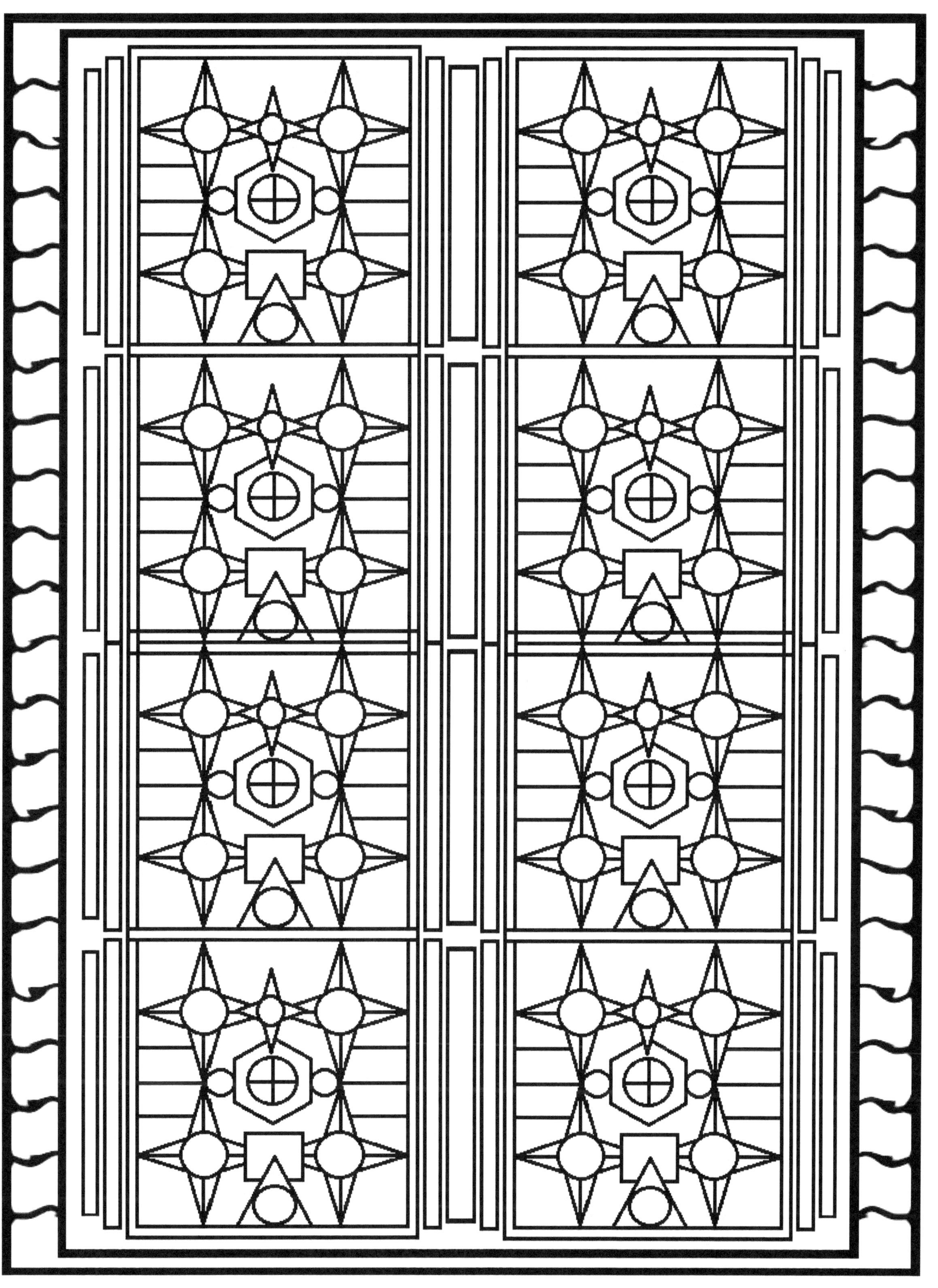

Bella Blue
Adult Coloring Book

find it on Amazon.com

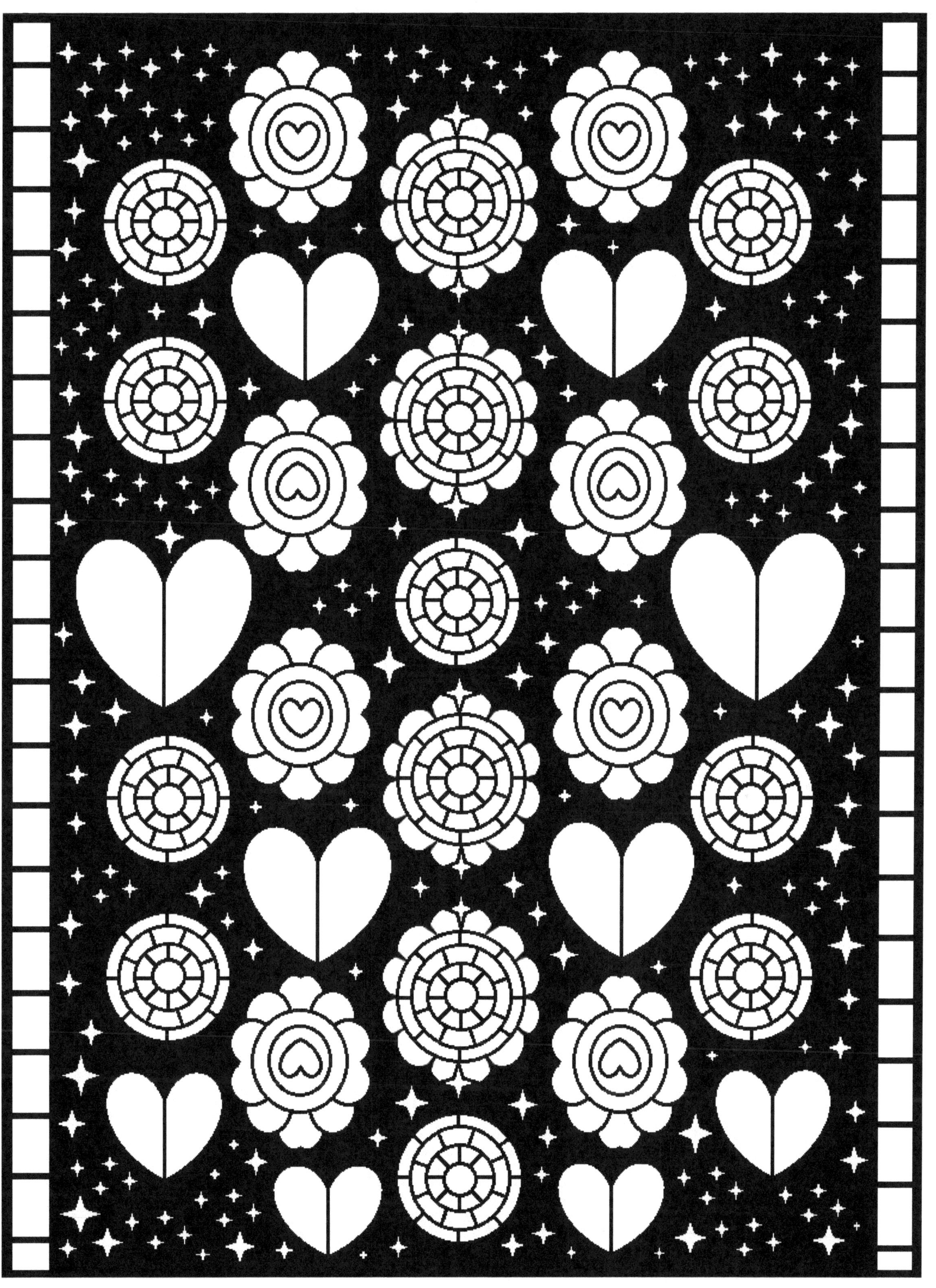

Bella Blue
Adult Coloring Book

find it on Amazon.com

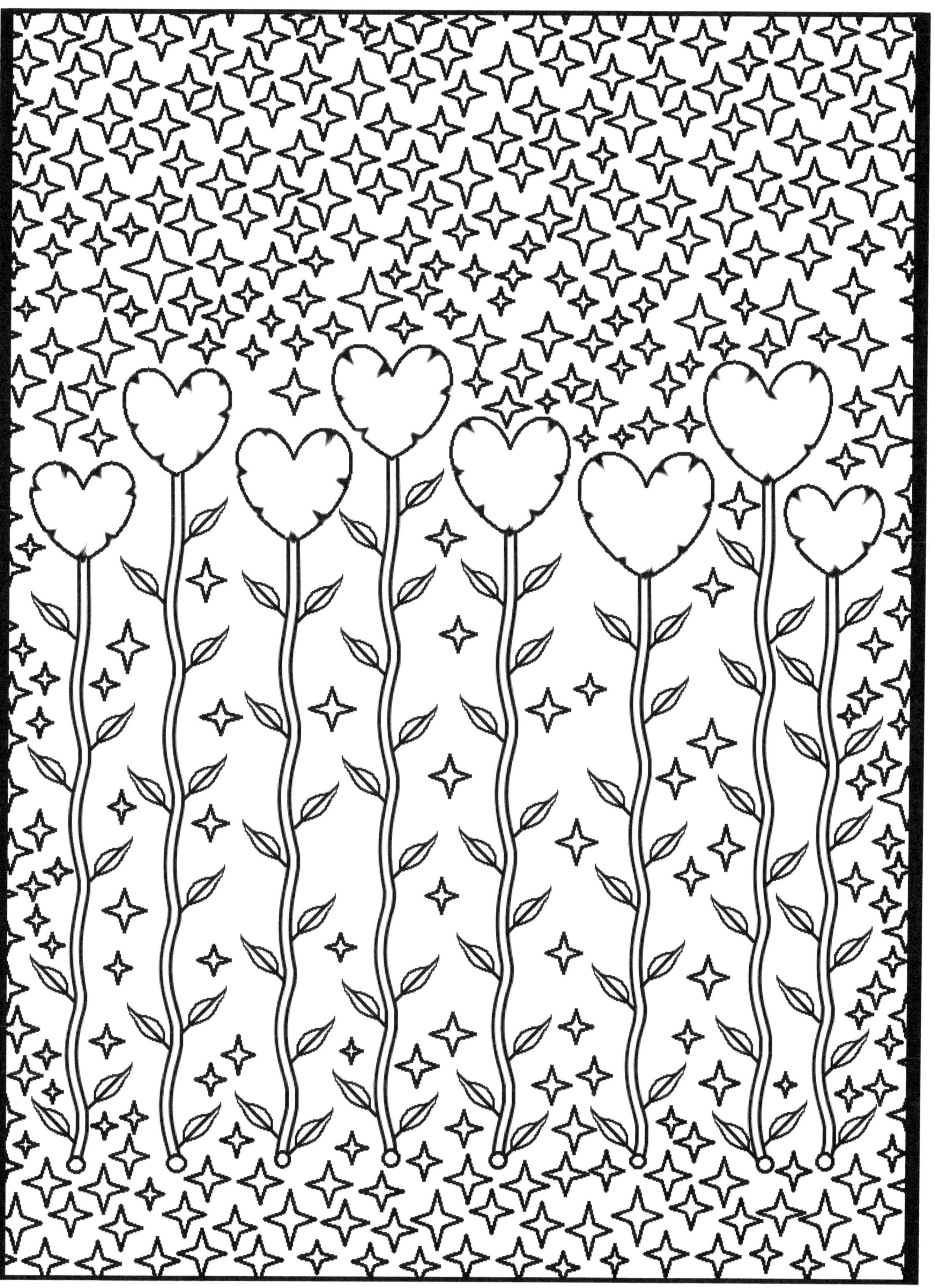

Bella Blue
Adult Coloring Book

find it on Amazon.com

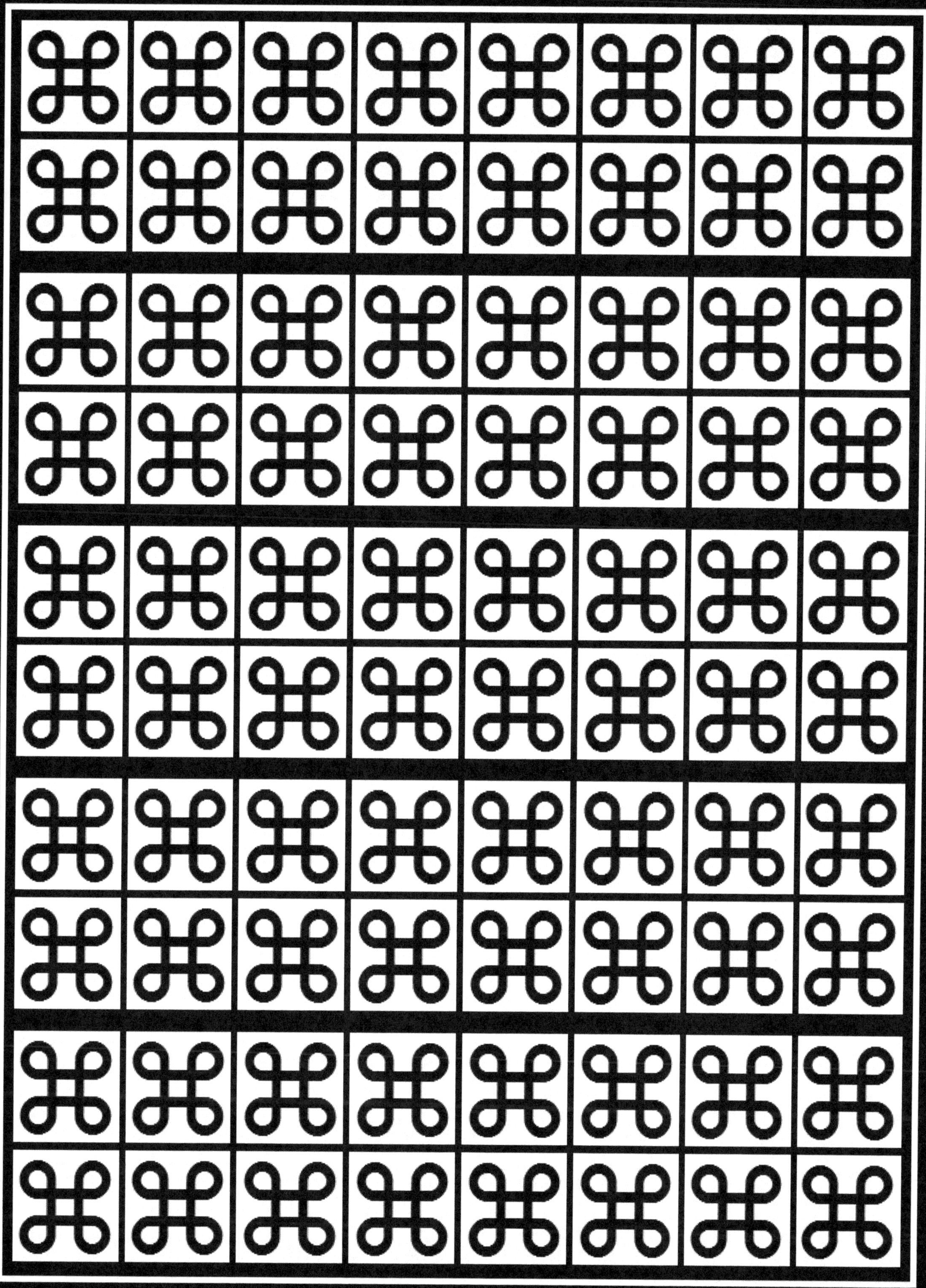

Bella Blue
Adult Coloring Book

find it on Amazon.com

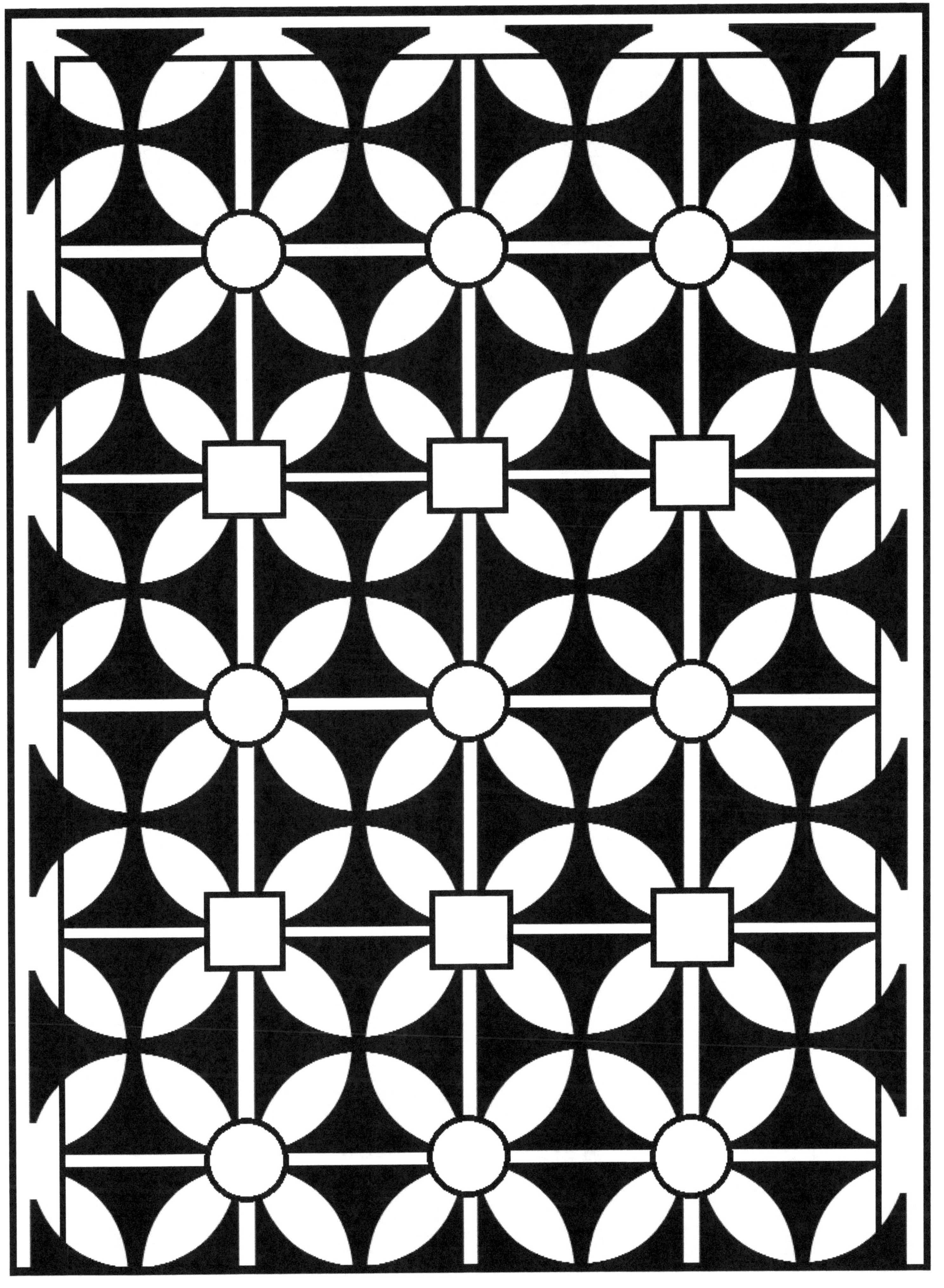

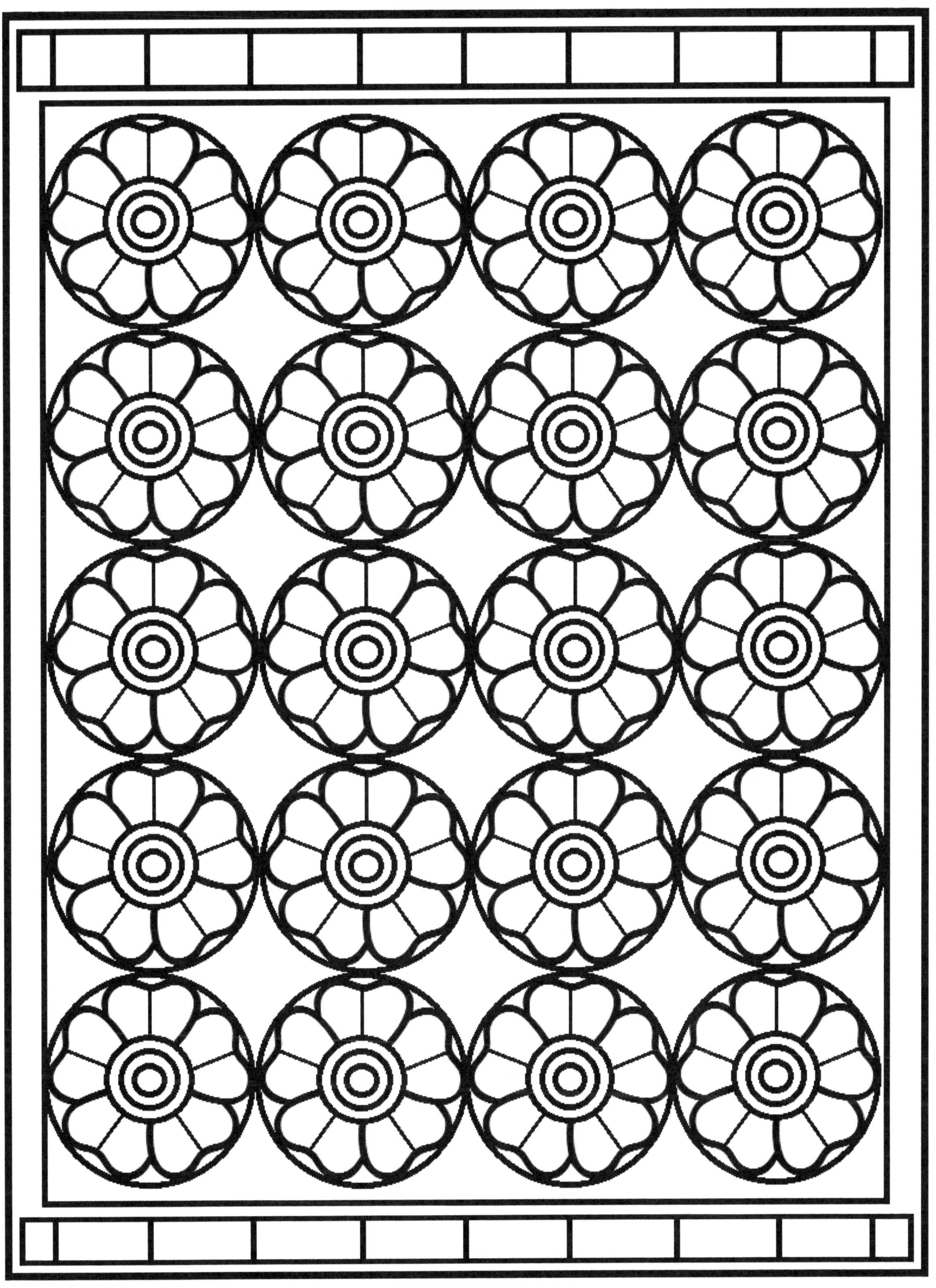

Bella Blue
Adult Coloring Book

find it on Amazon.com

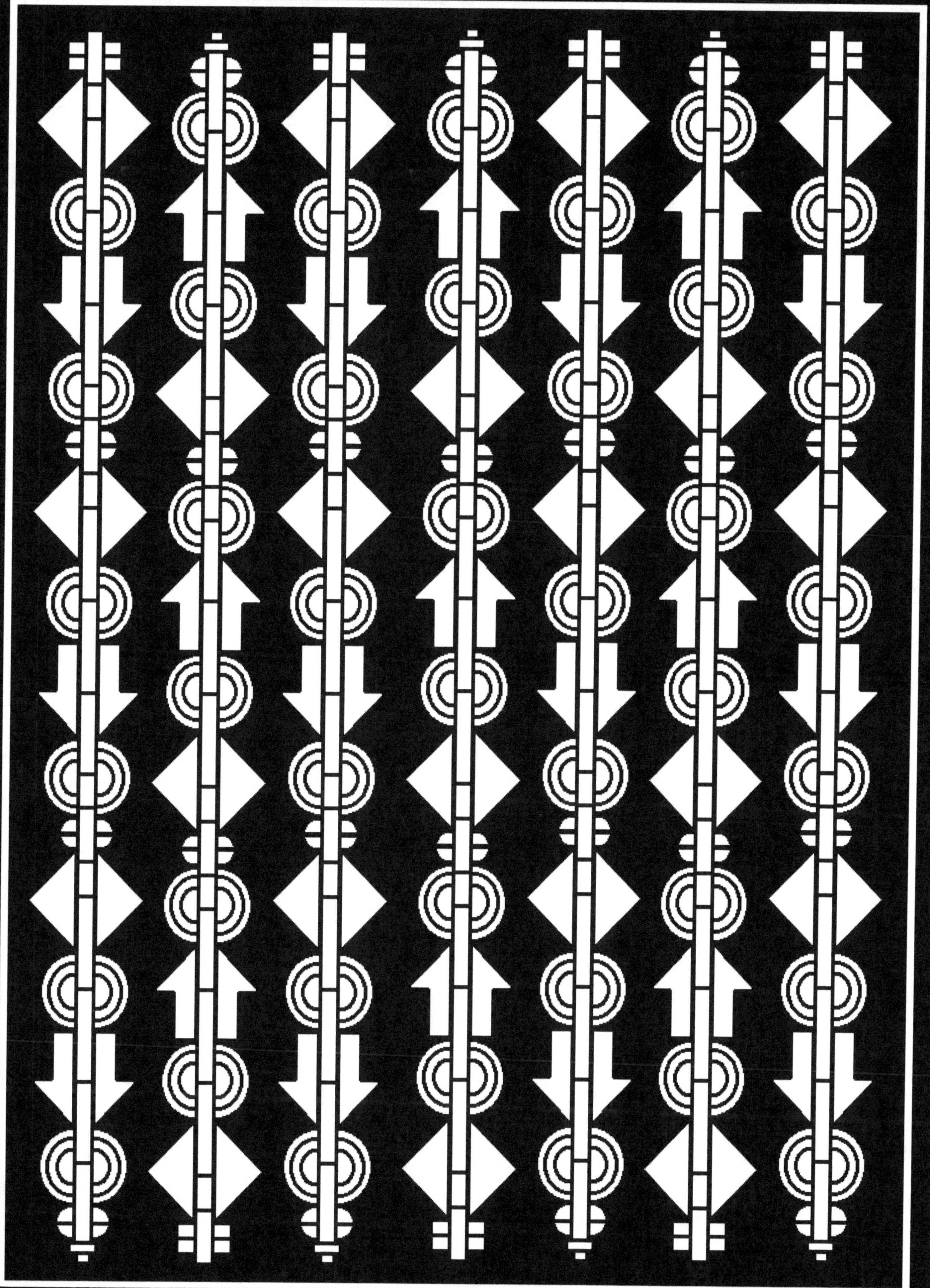

Bella Blue
Adult Coloring Book

find it on Amazon.com

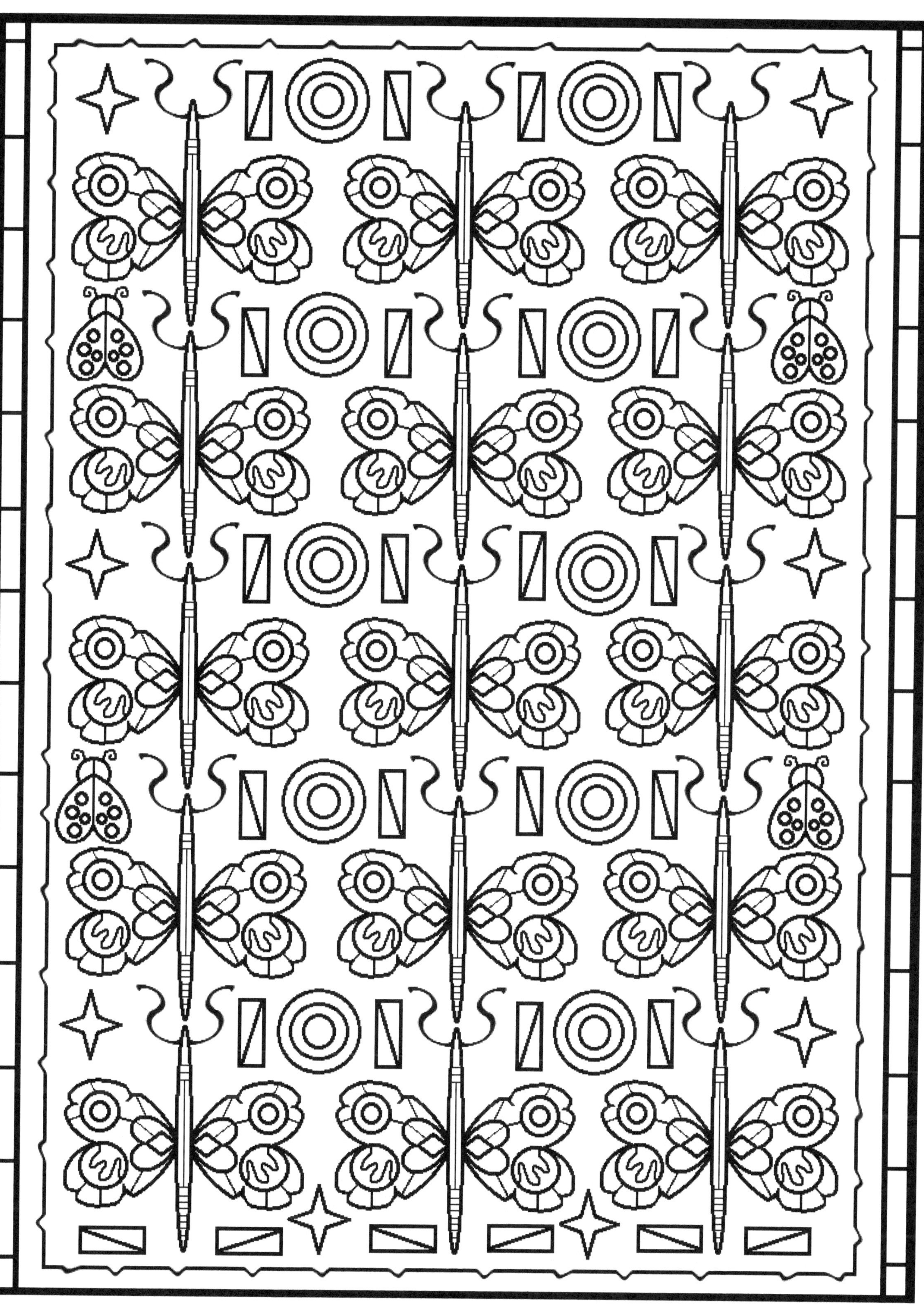

Bella Blue
Adult Coloring Book

find it on Amazon.com

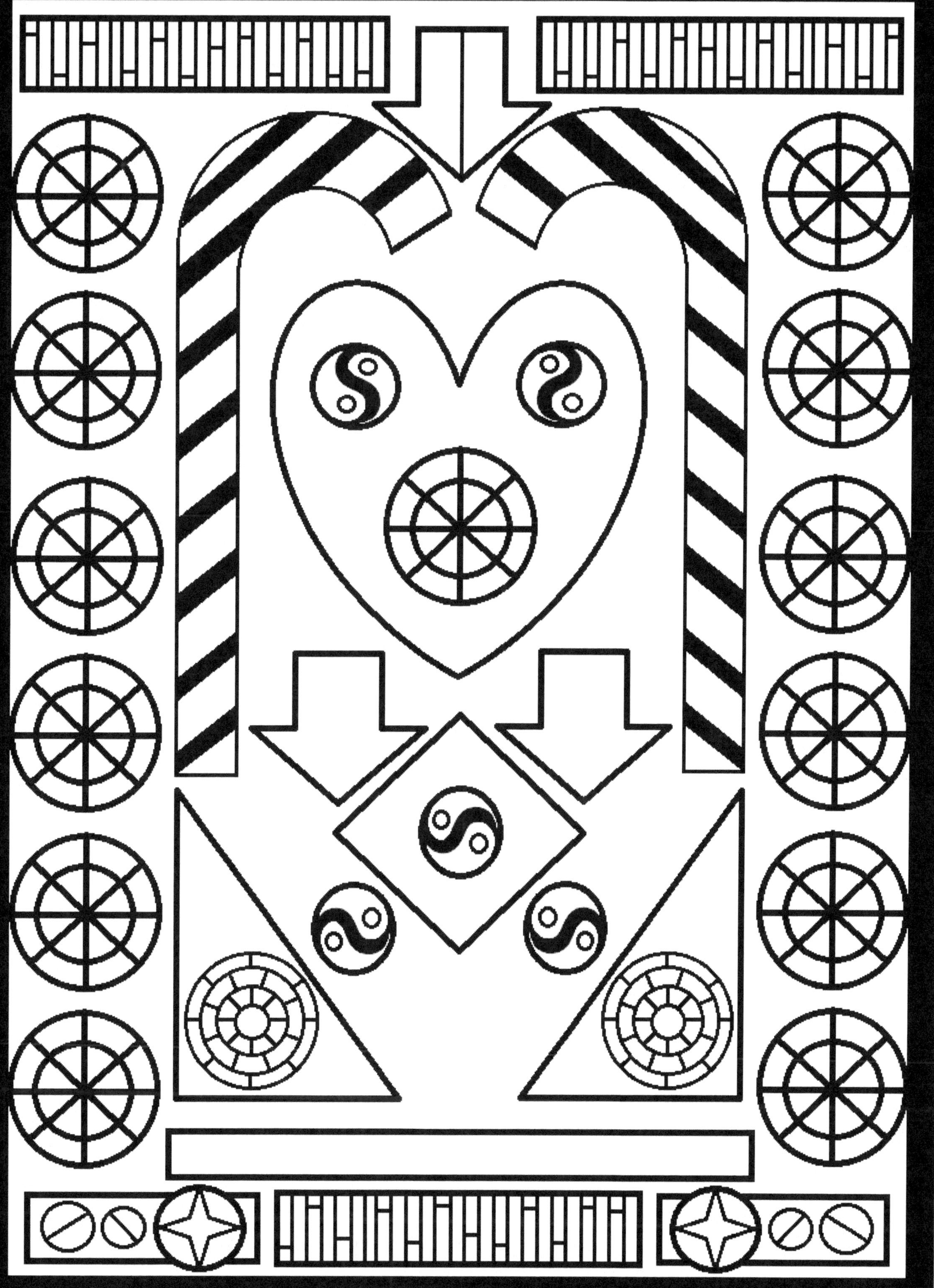

Bella Blue
Adult Coloring Book

find it on Amazon.com

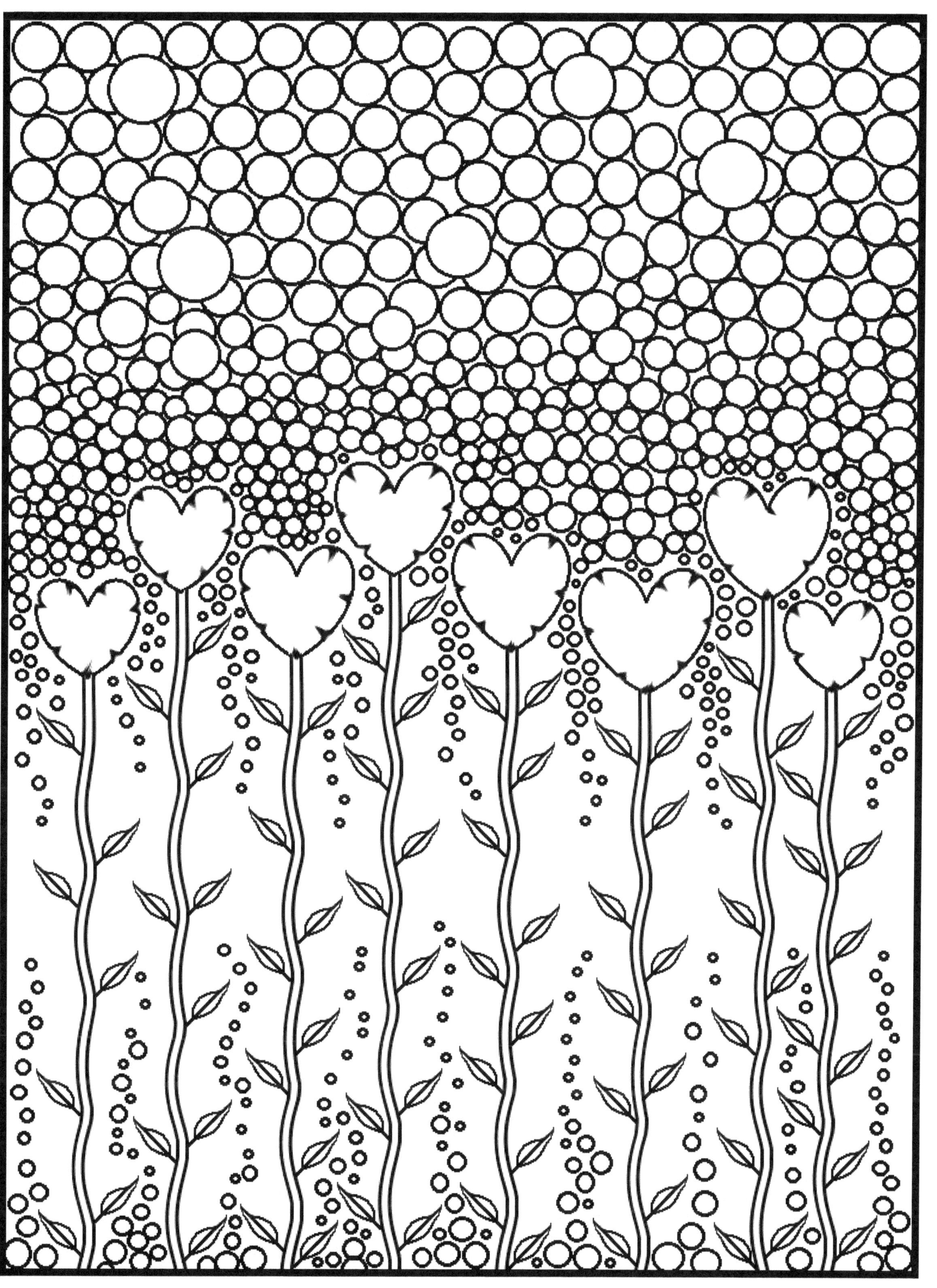

Bella Blue
Adult Coloring Book

find it on Amazon.com

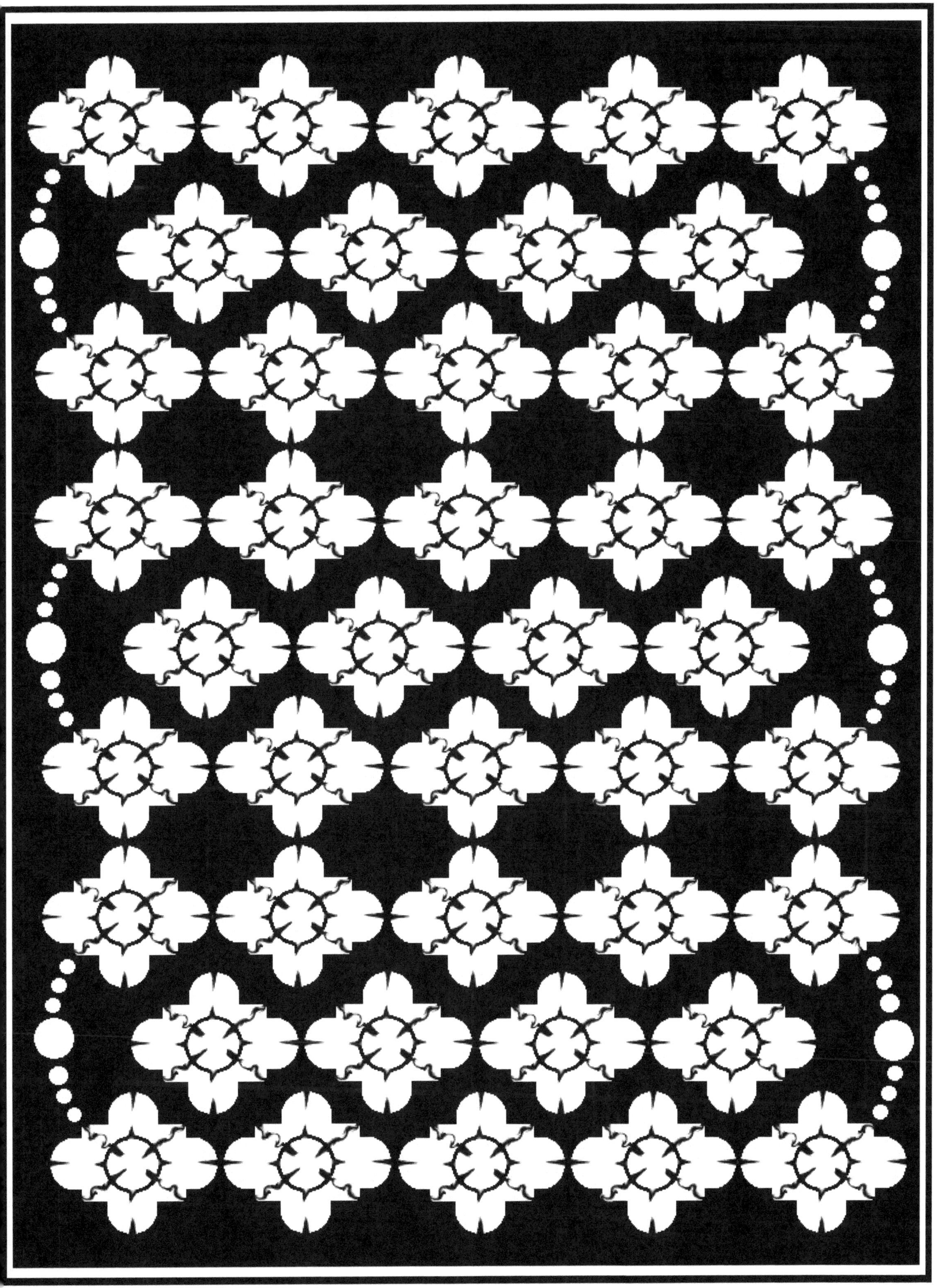

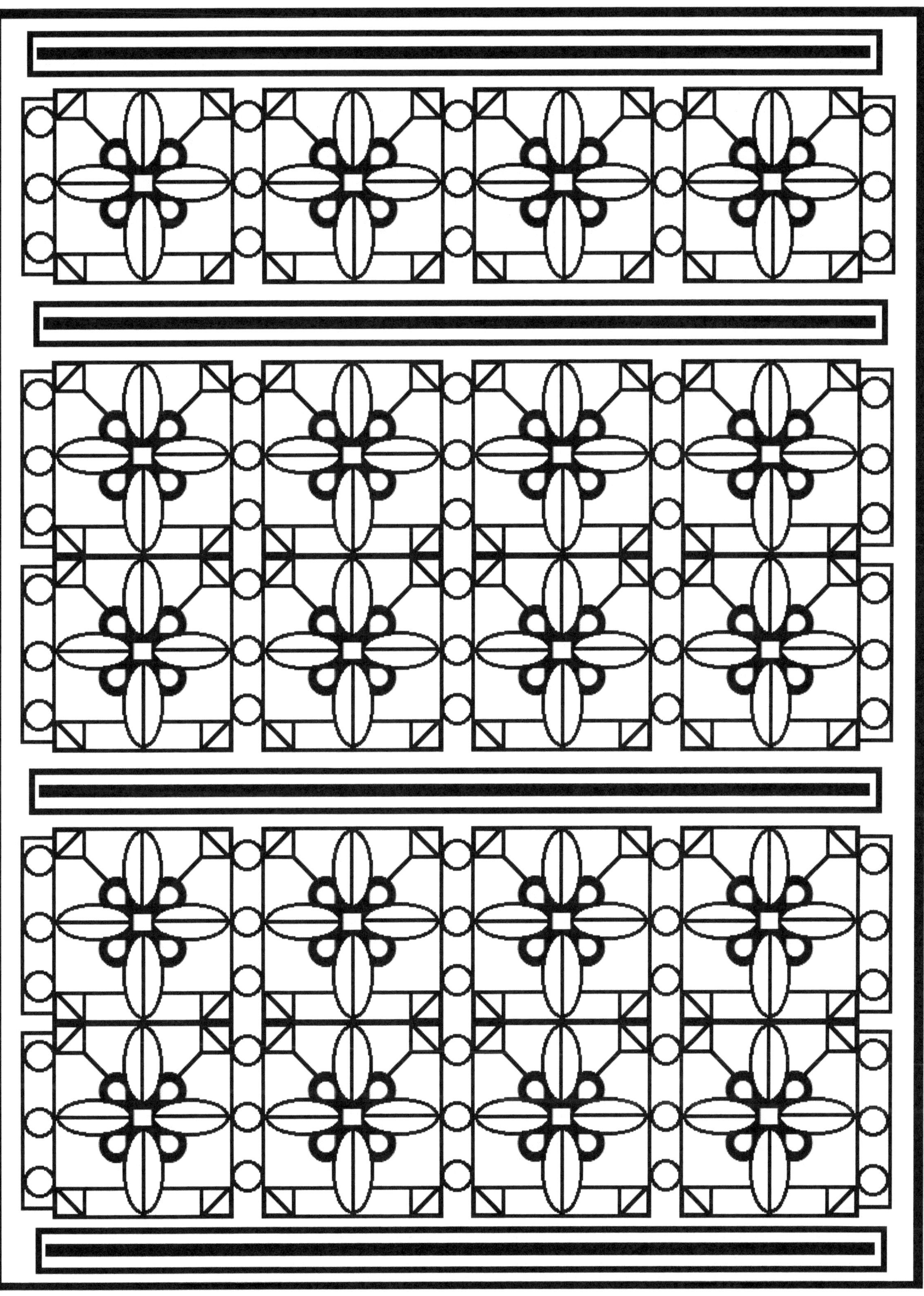

Bella Blue
Adult Coloring Book

find it on Amazon.com

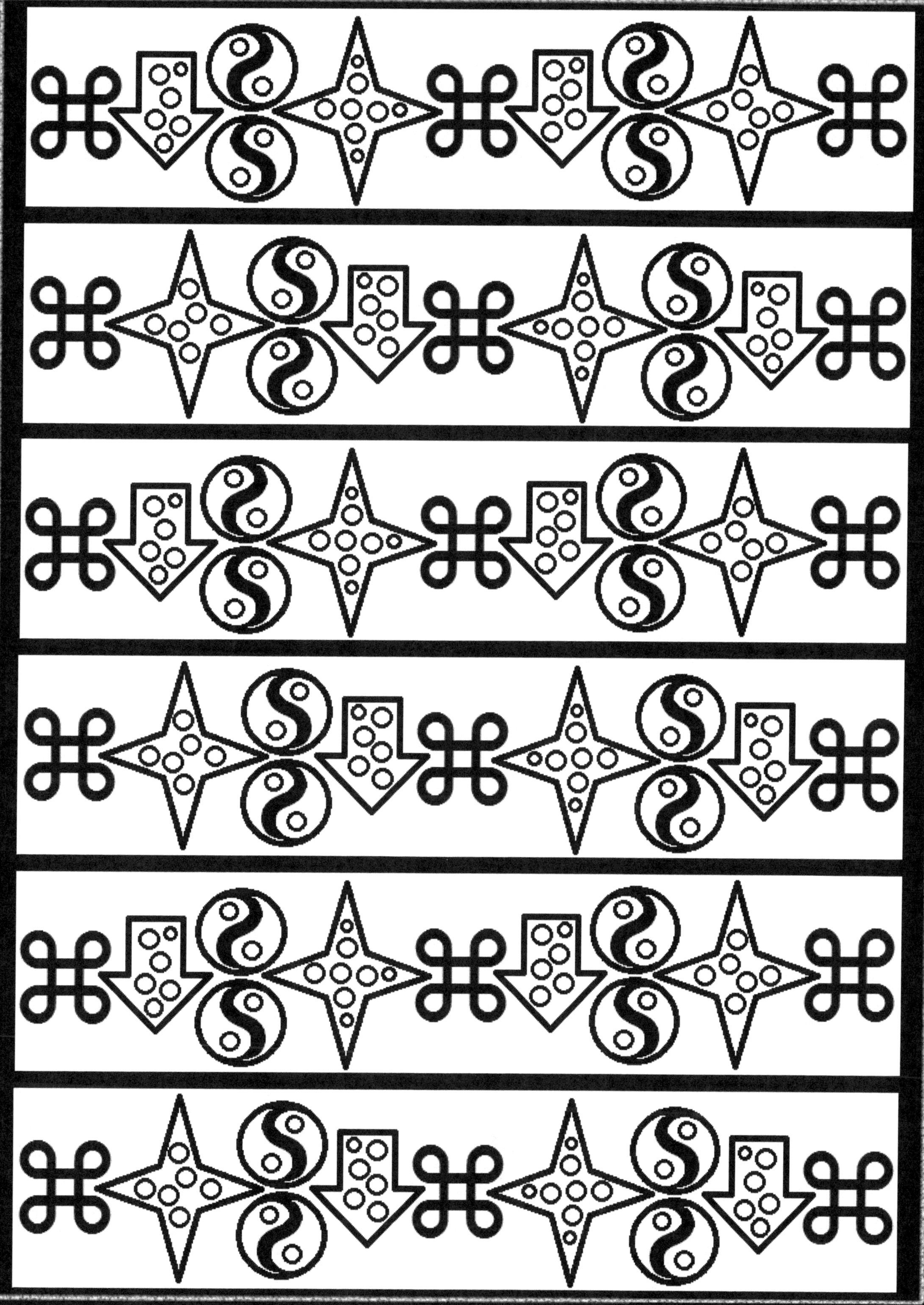

Bella Blue

Adult Coloring Book

find it on Amazon.com

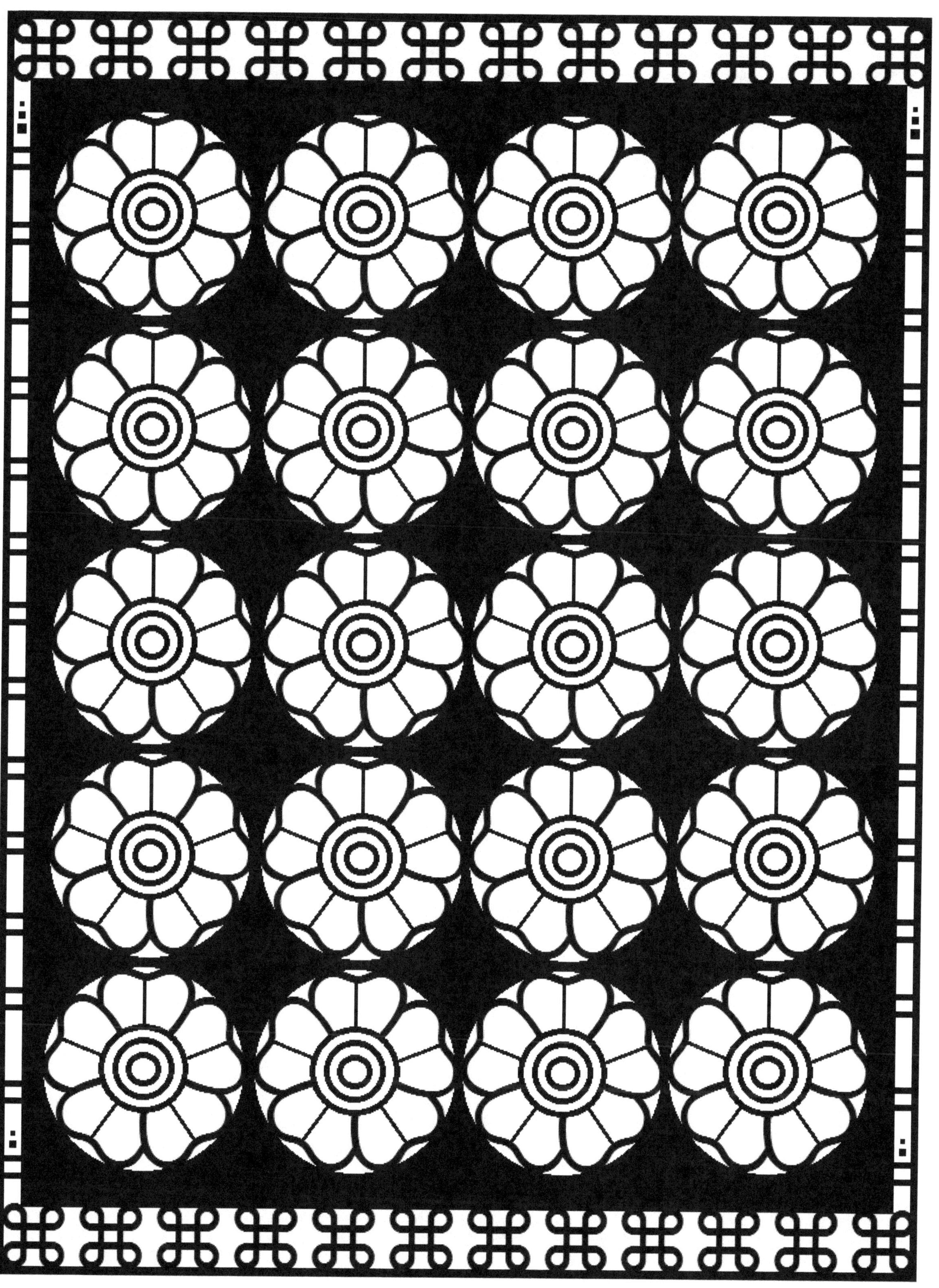

Bella Blue
Adult Coloring Book

find it on Amazon.com

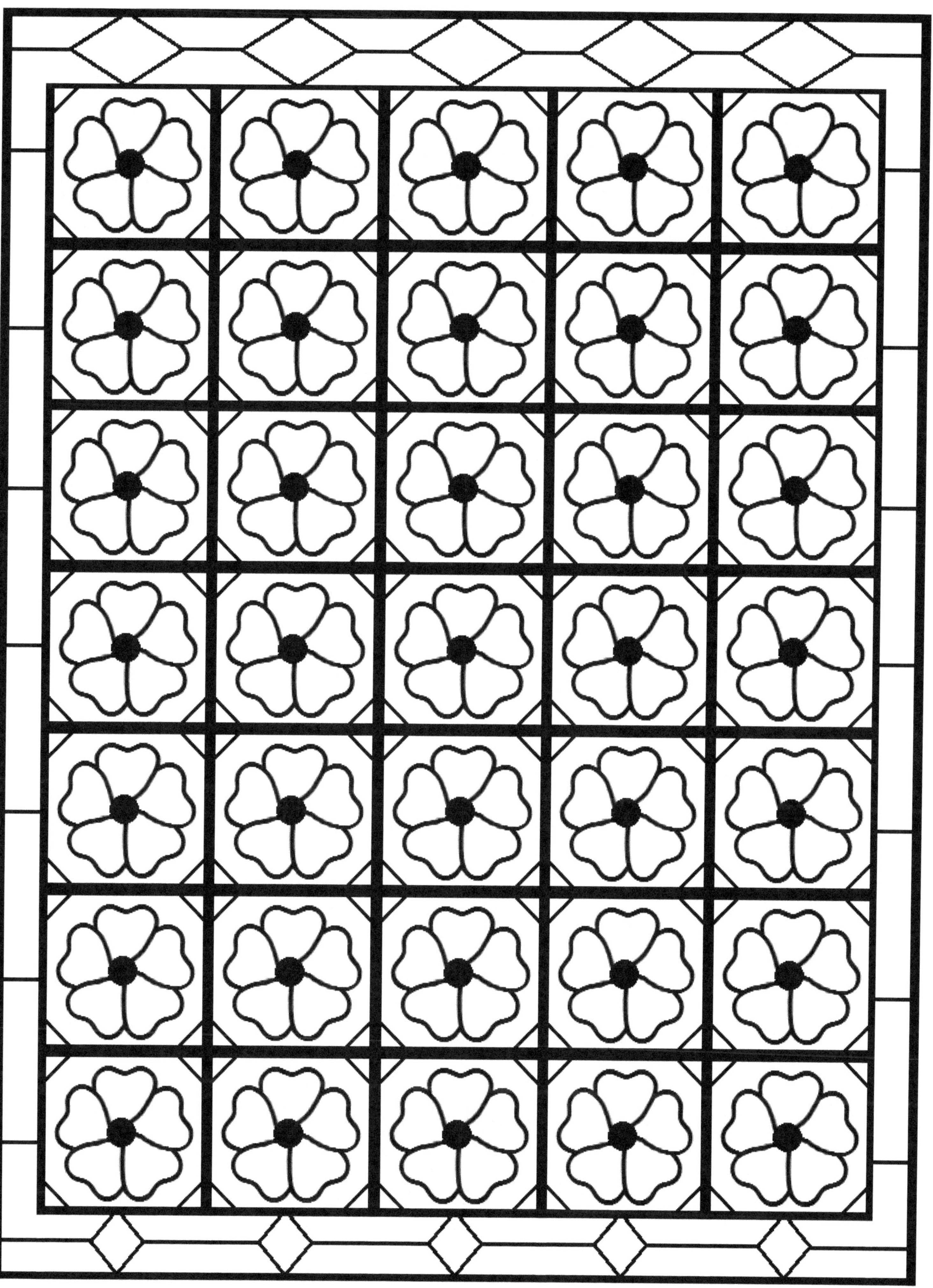

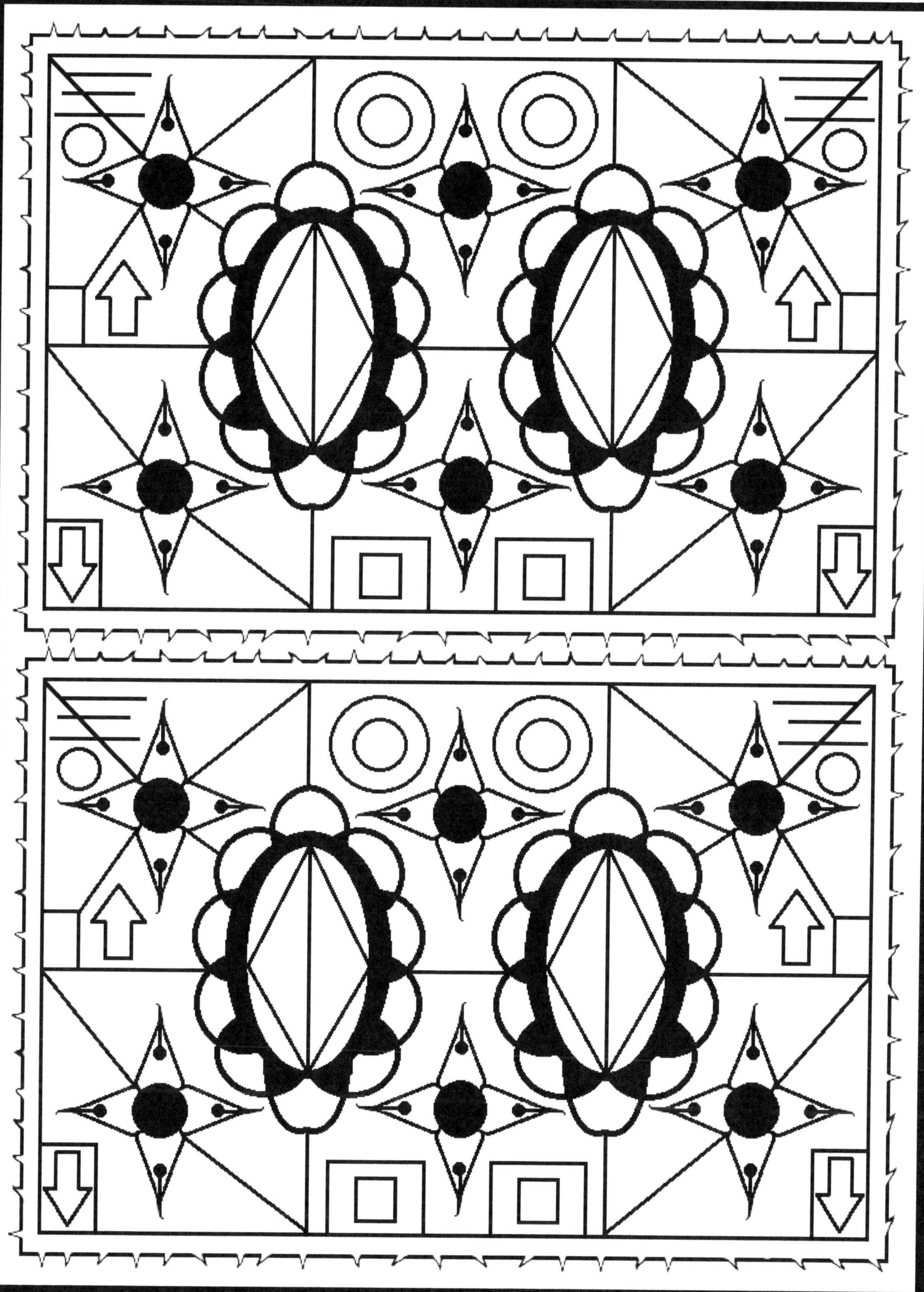

Bella Blue
Adult Coloring Book

find it on Amazon.com

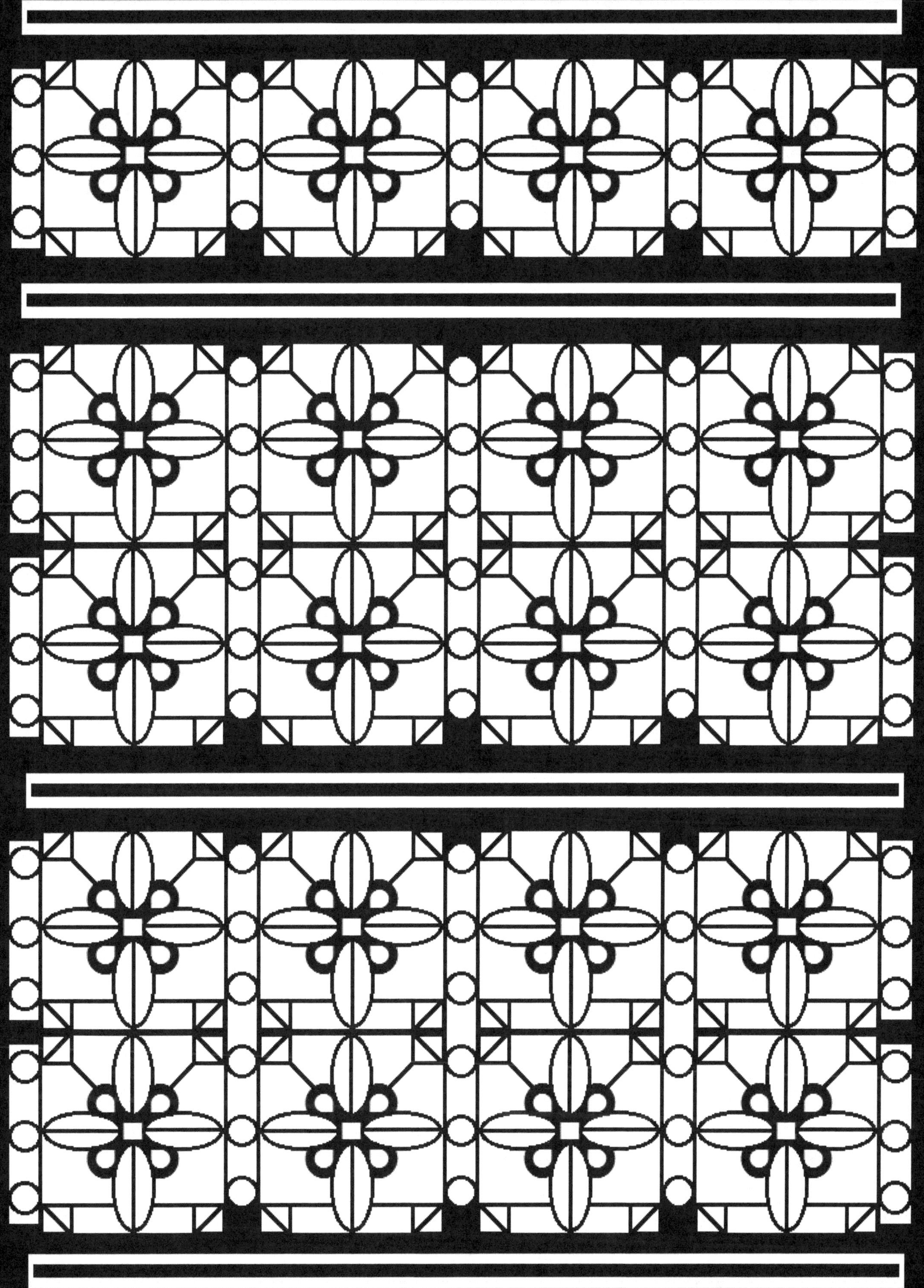

Bella Blue
Adult Coloring Book

find it on Amazon.com

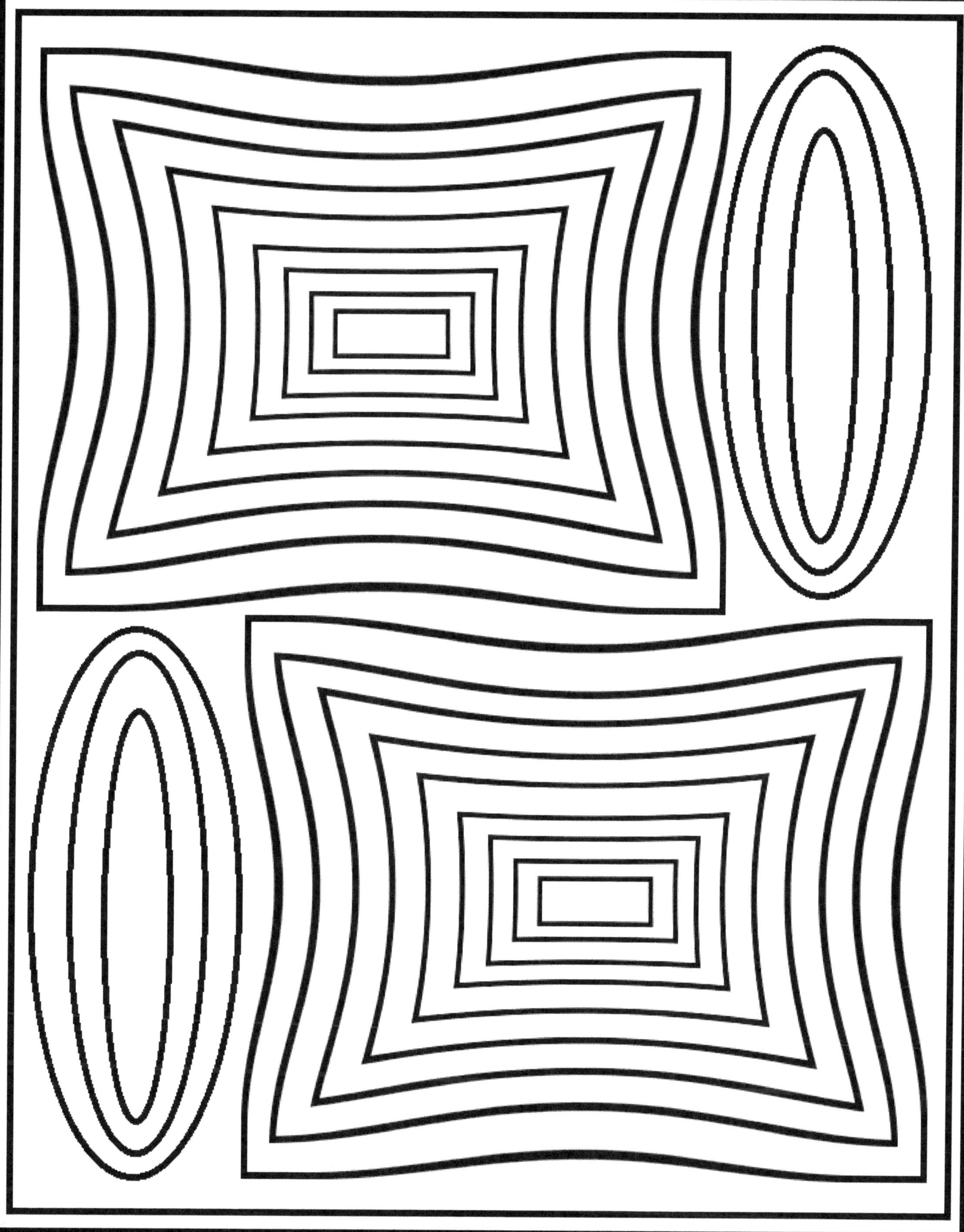

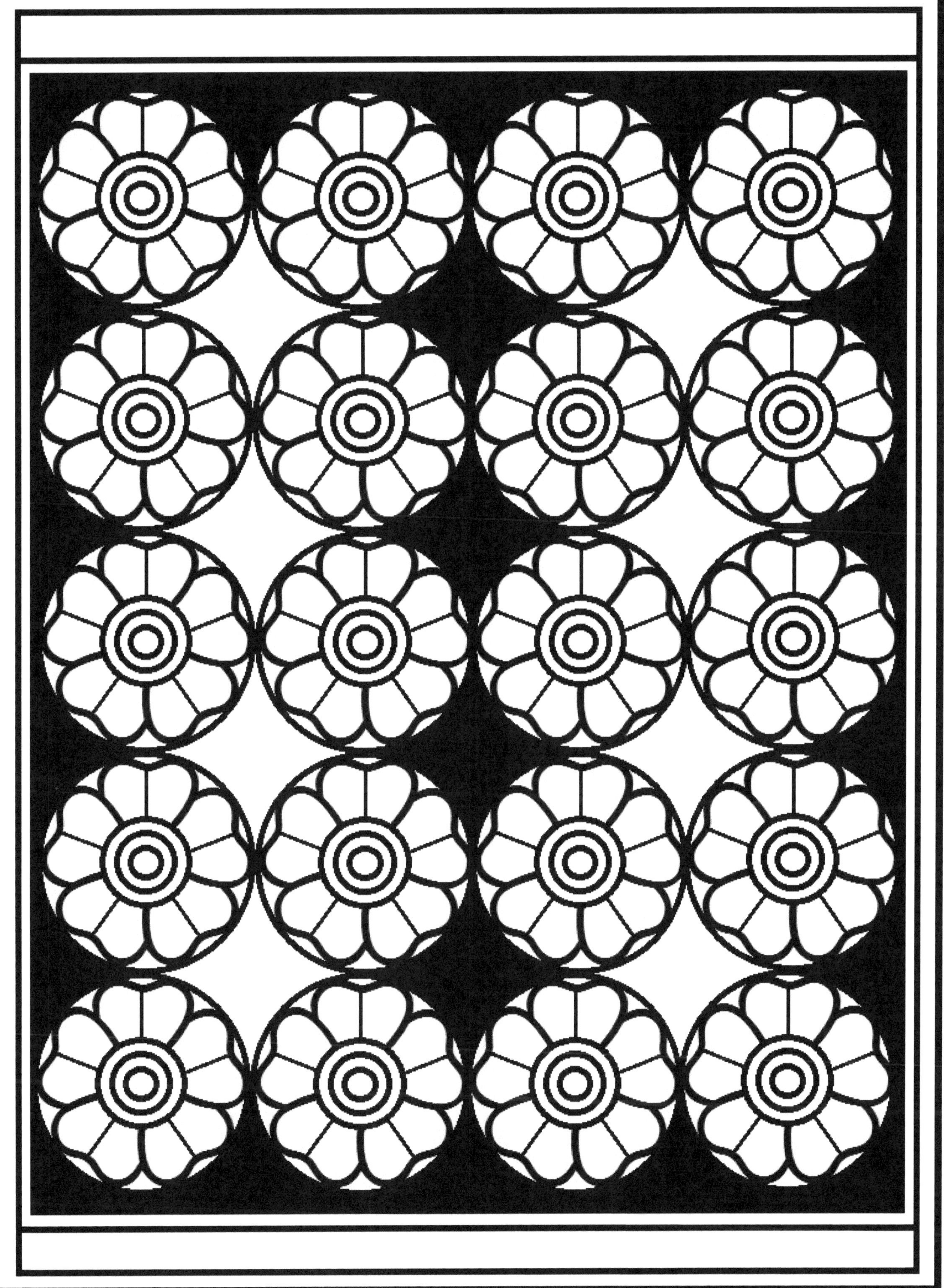

Bella Blue
Adult Coloring Book

find it on Amazon.com

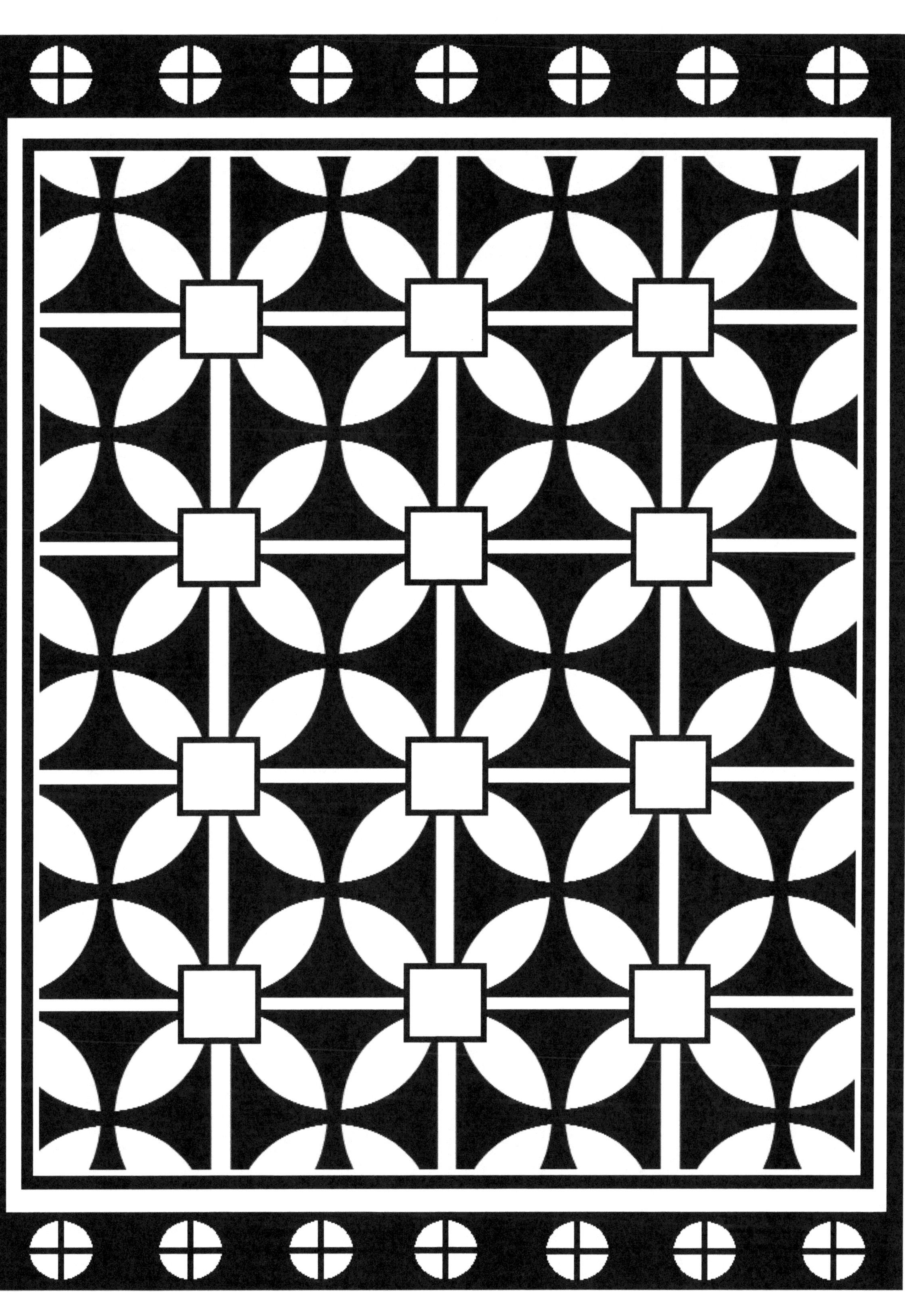

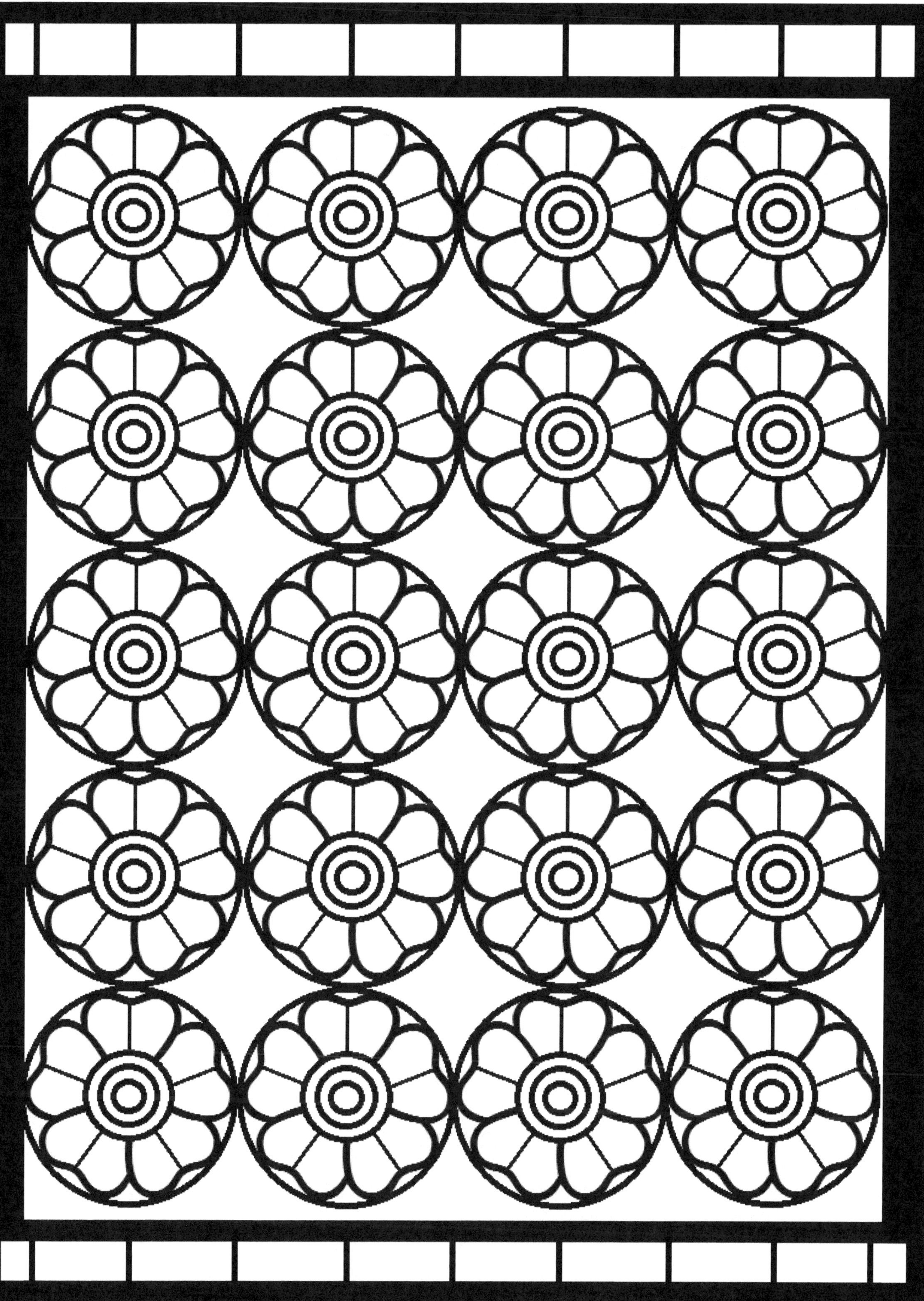

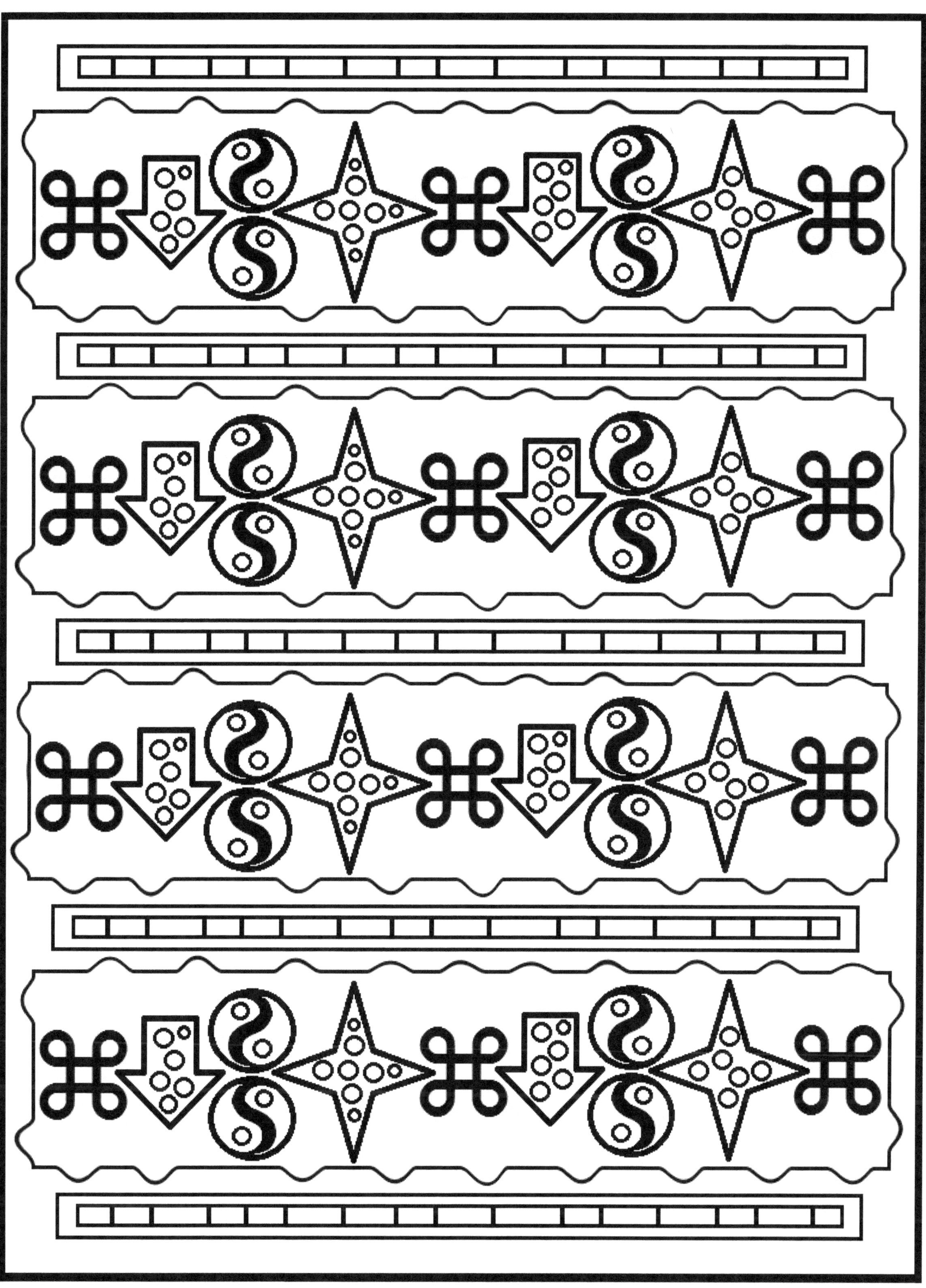

Bella Blue
Adult Coloring Book

find it on Amazon.com

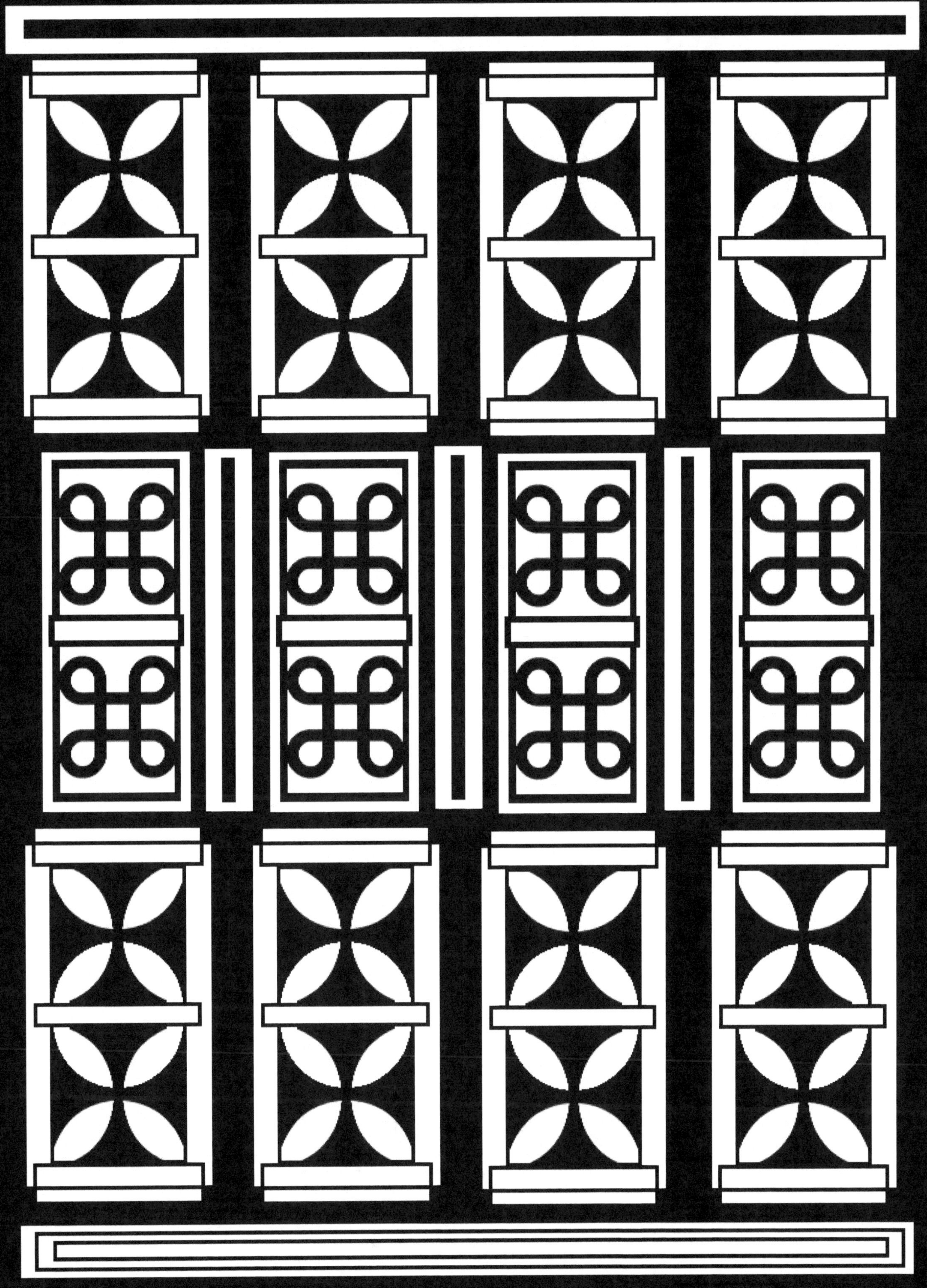

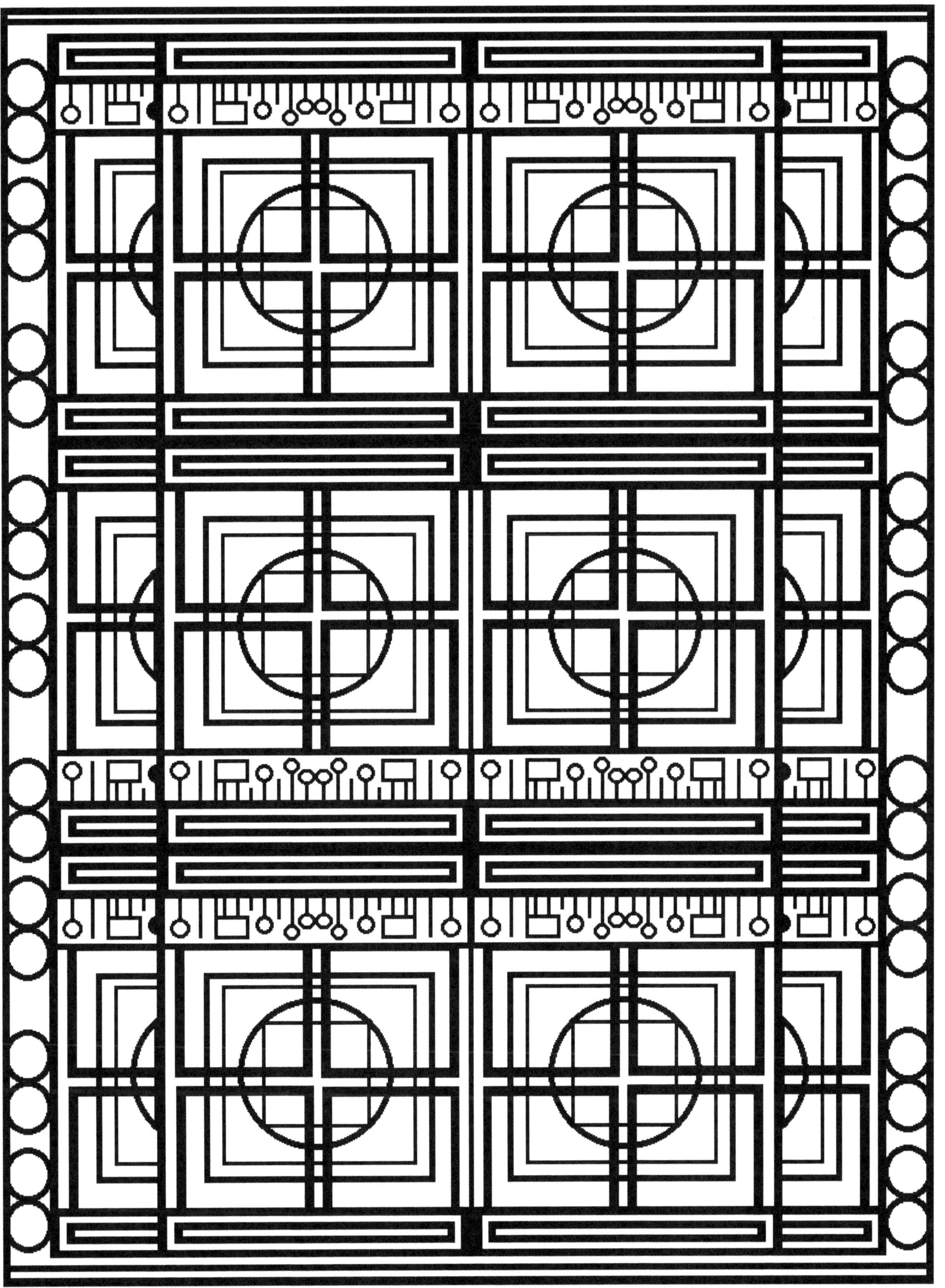

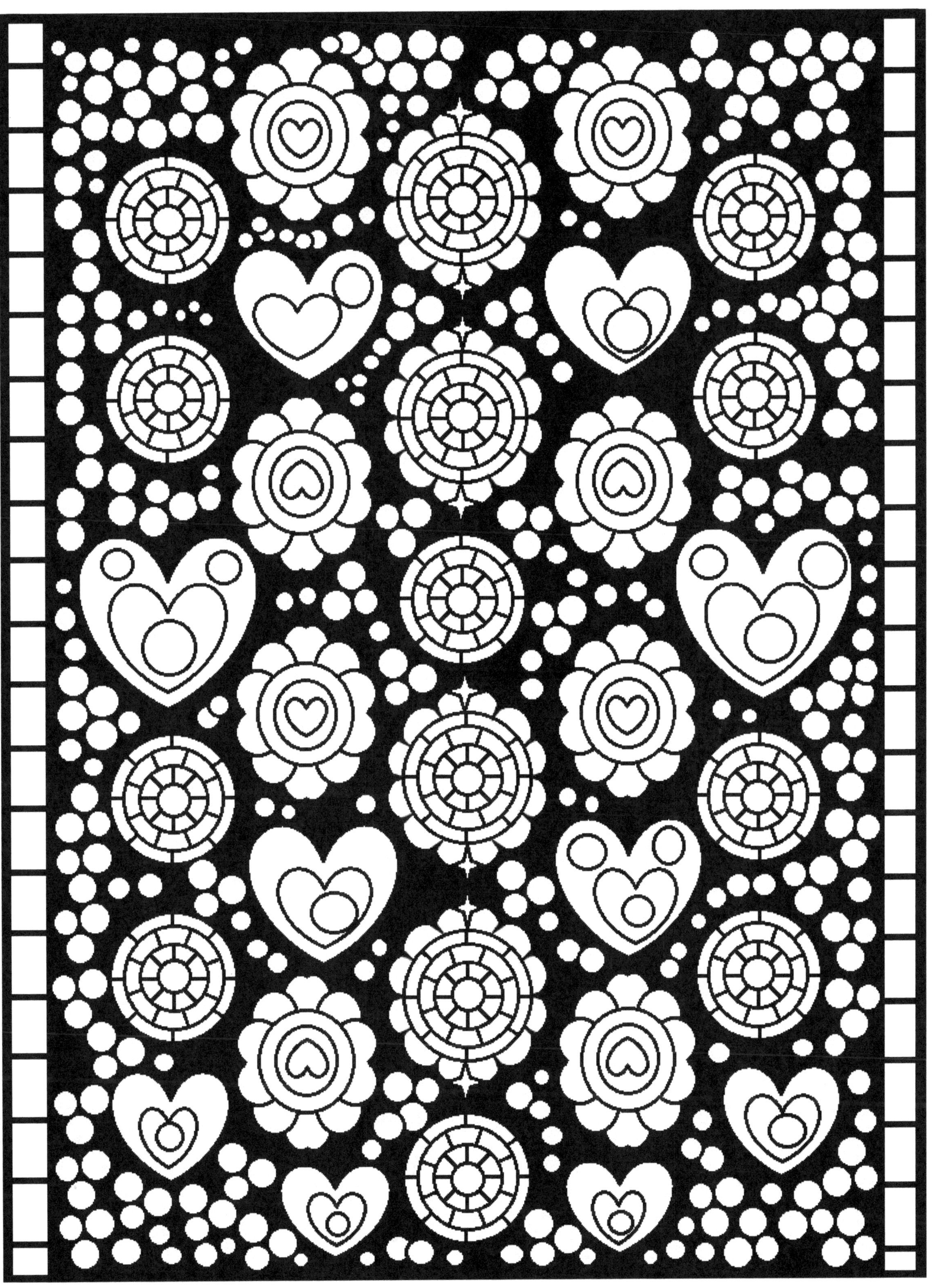

Bella Blue
Adult Coloring Book

find it on Amazon.com

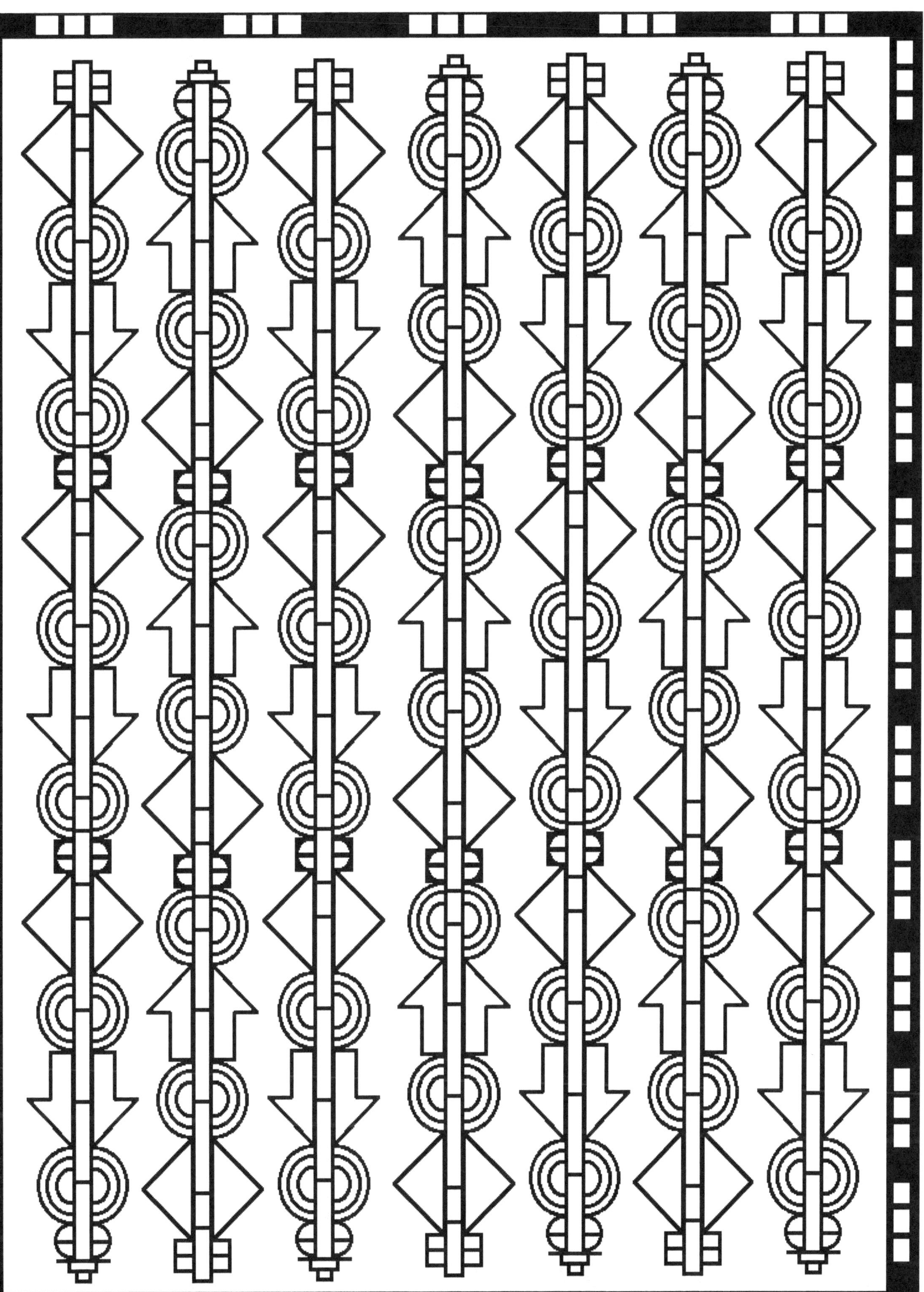

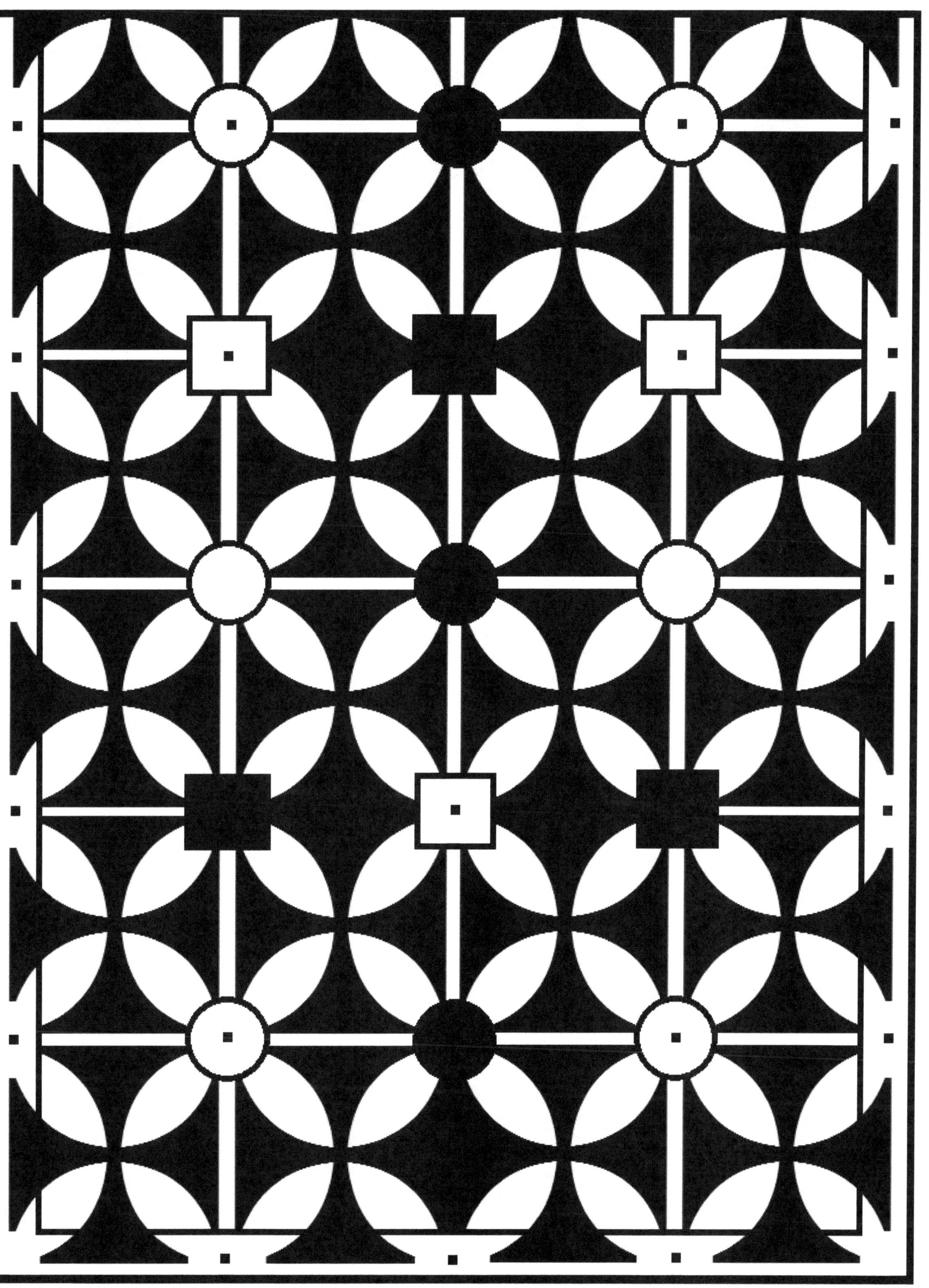

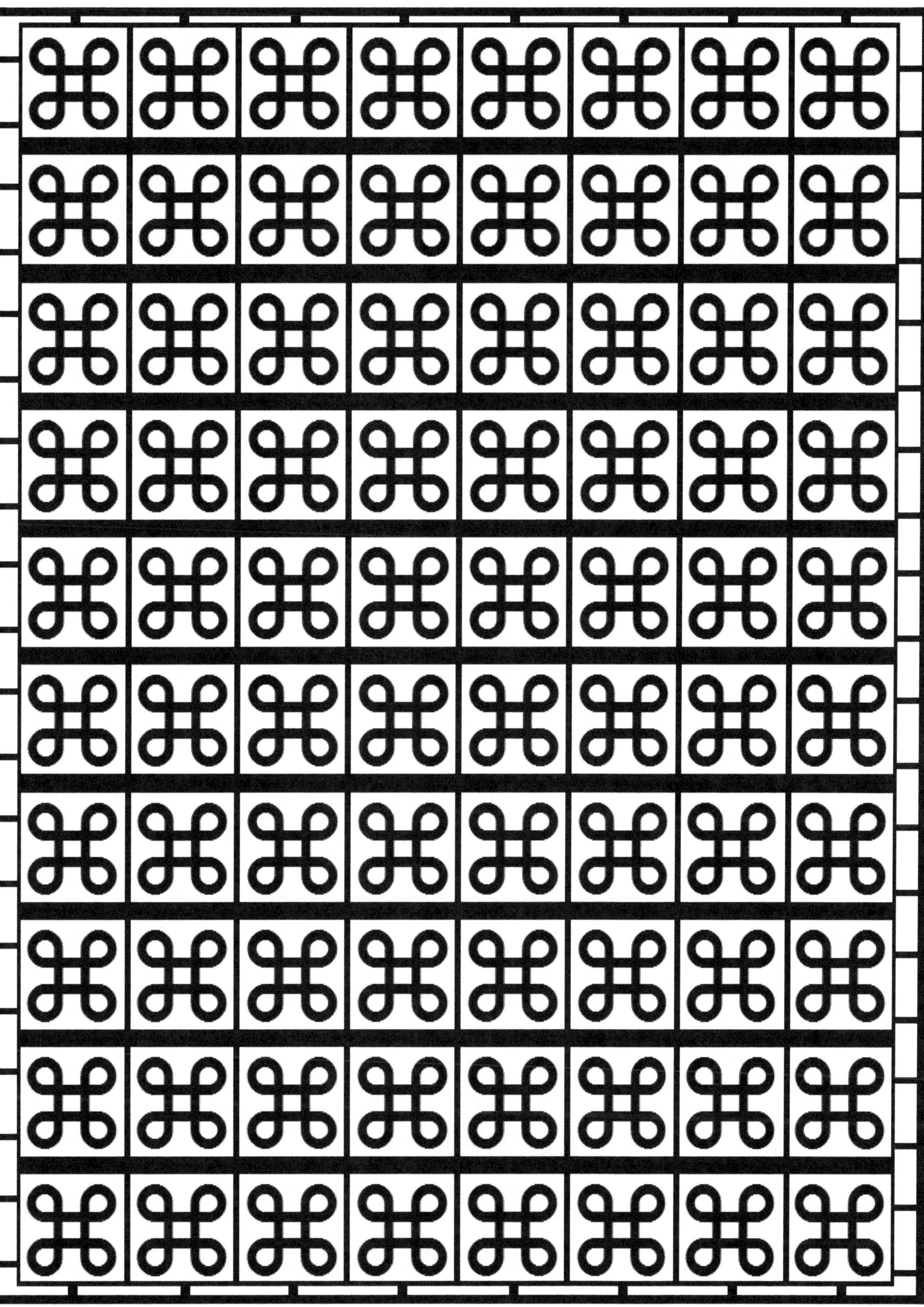

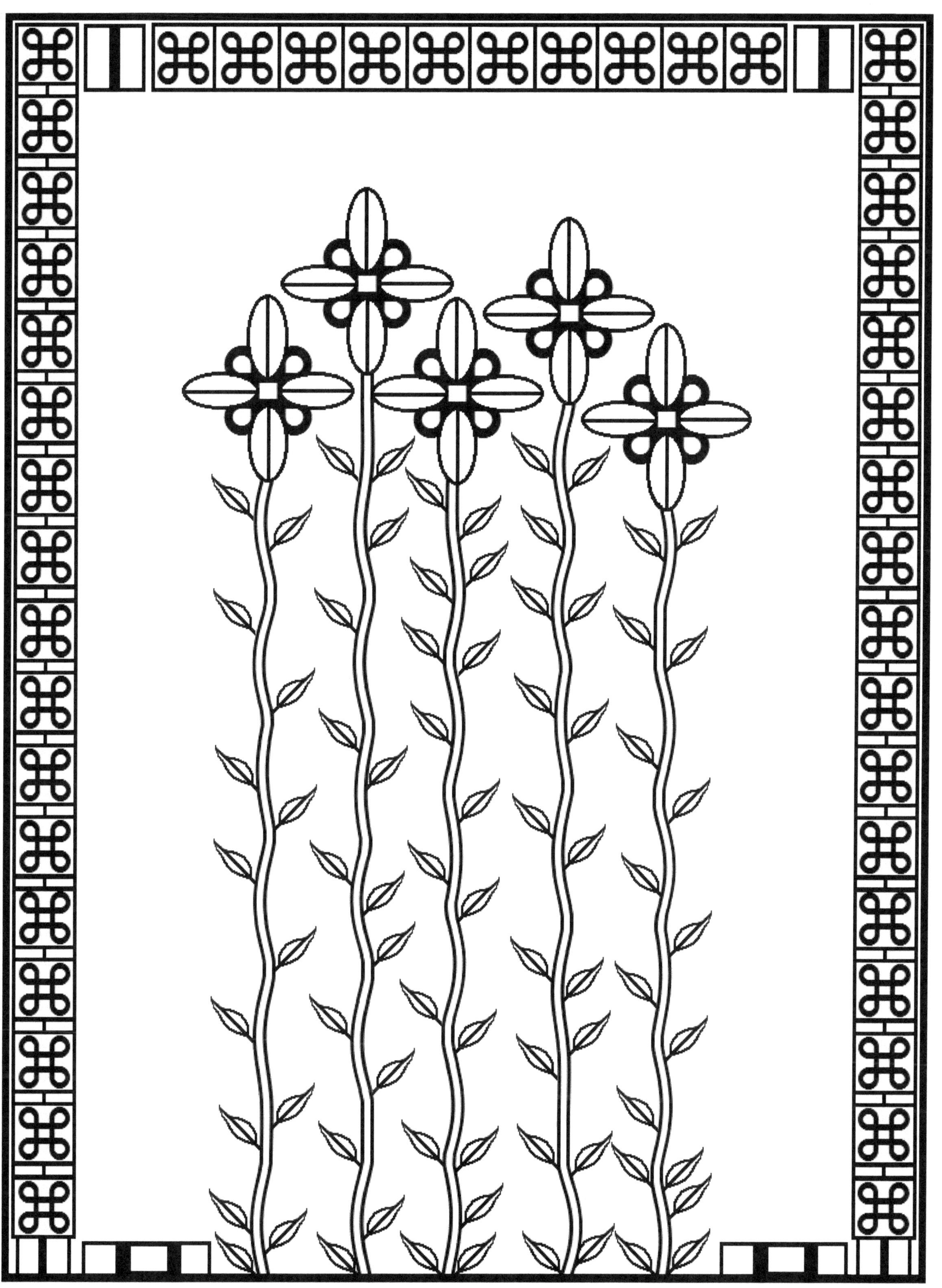

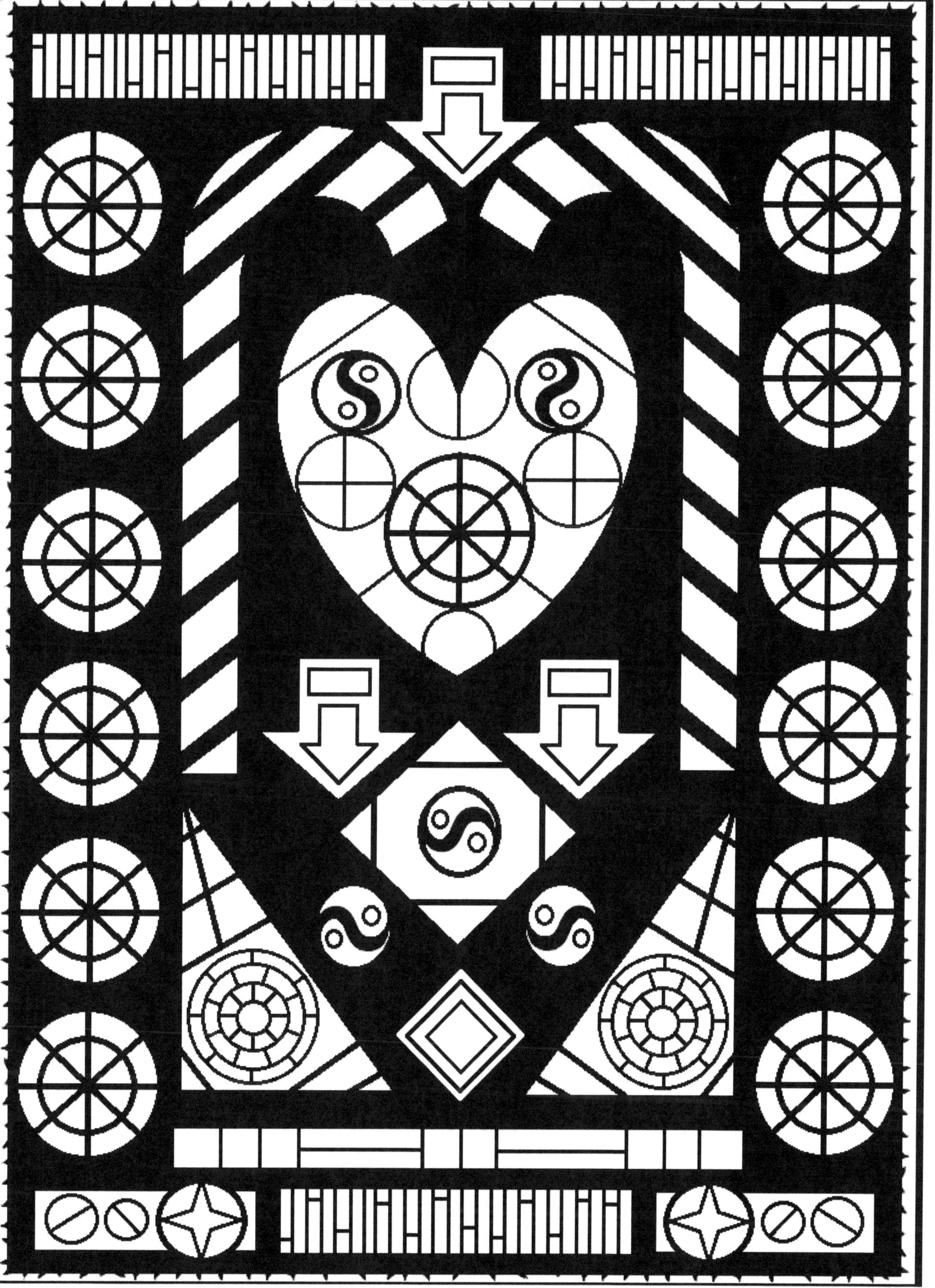

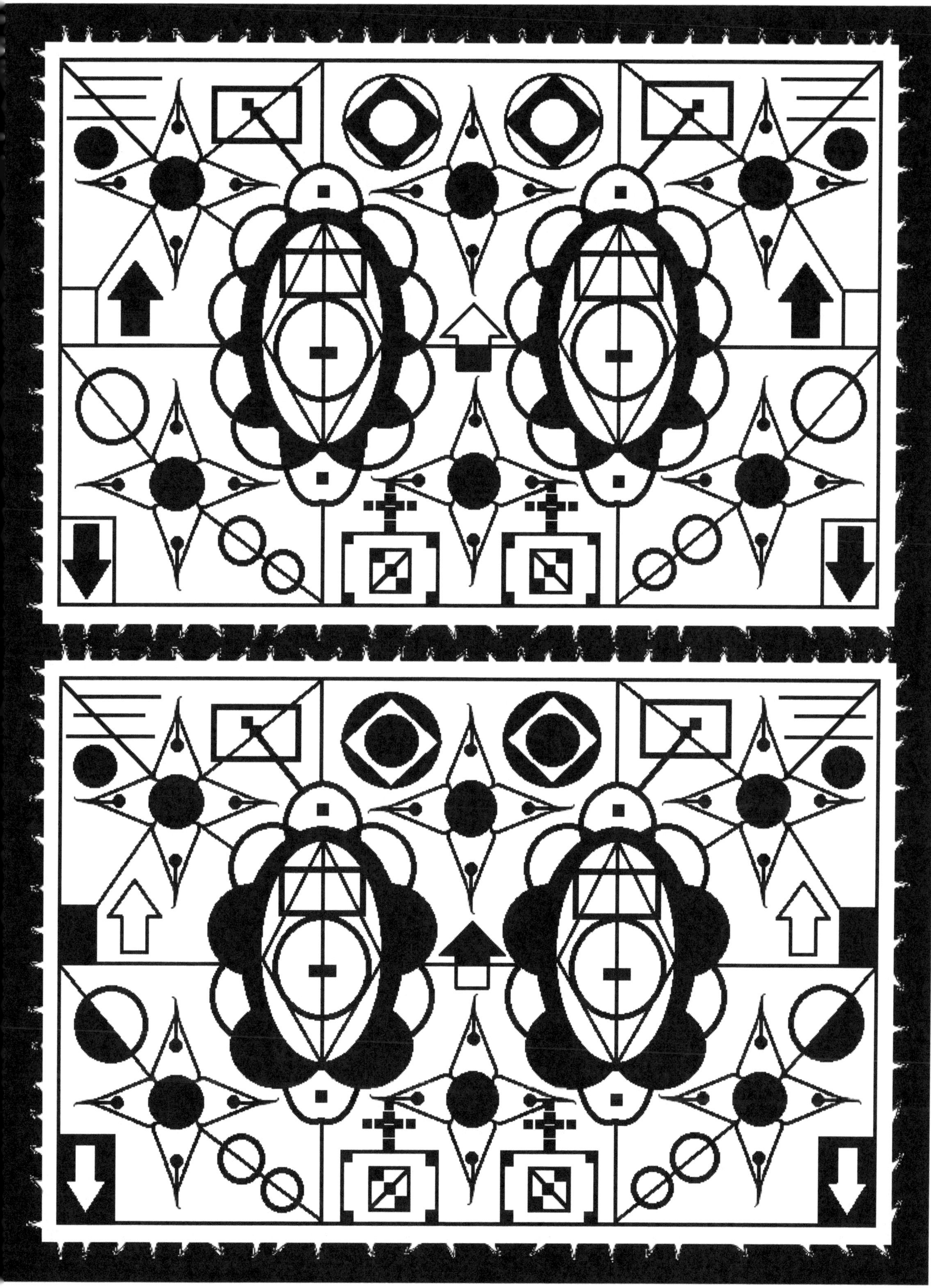

Bella Blue
Adult Coloring Book

find it on Amazon.com

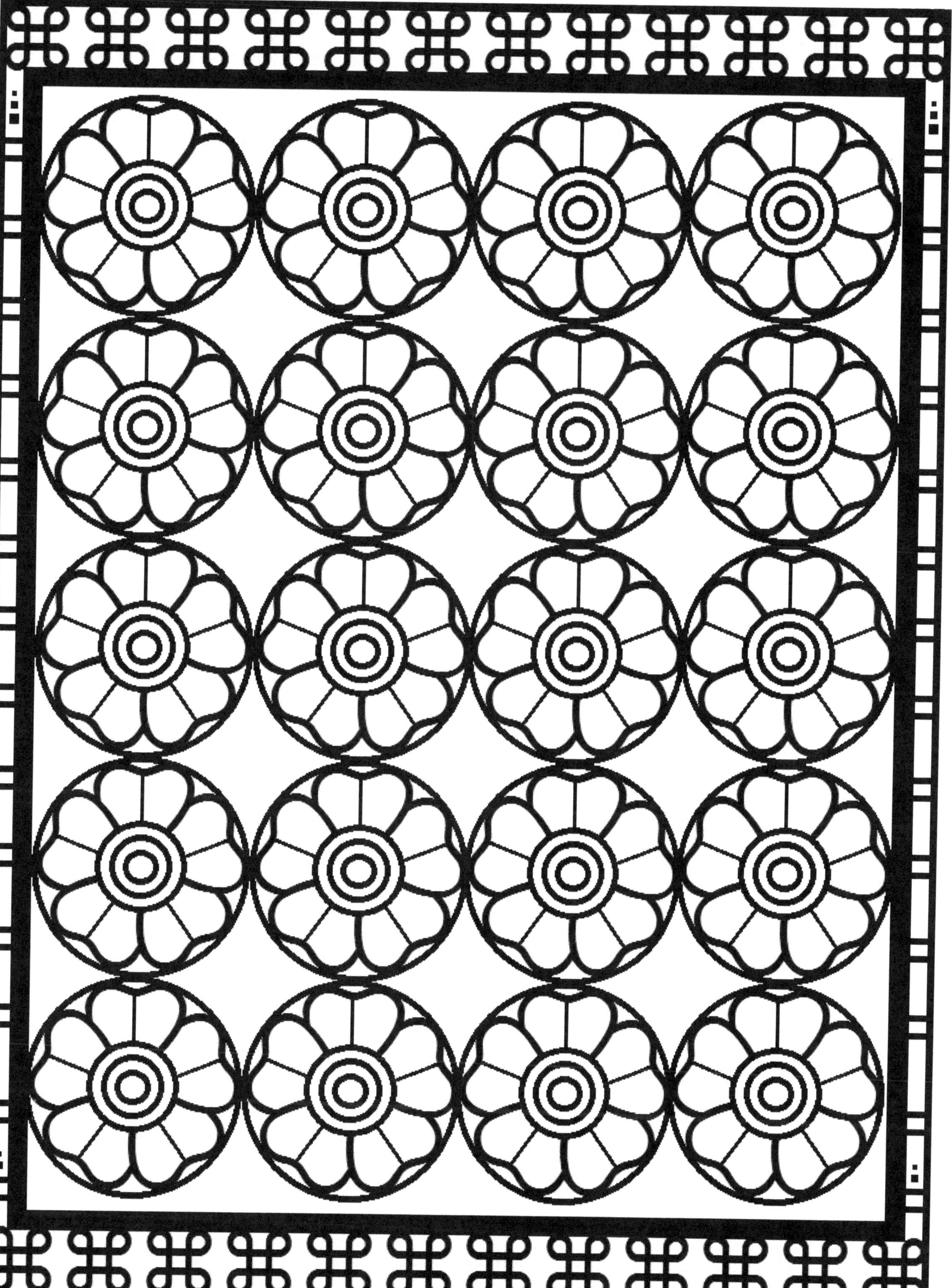

Bella Blue
Adult Coloring Book

find it on Amazon.com

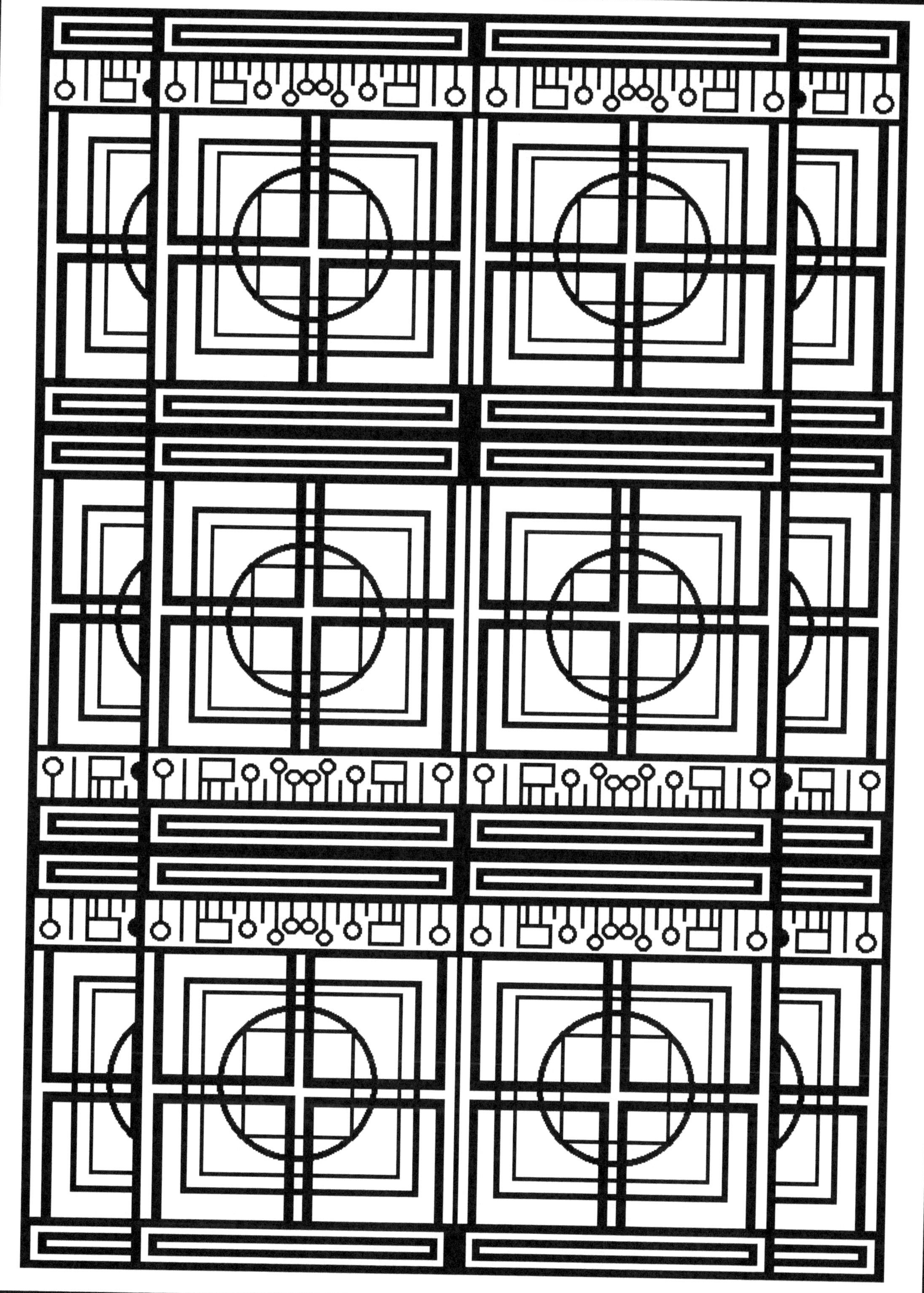

Bella Blue
Adult Coloring Book

find it on Amazon.com

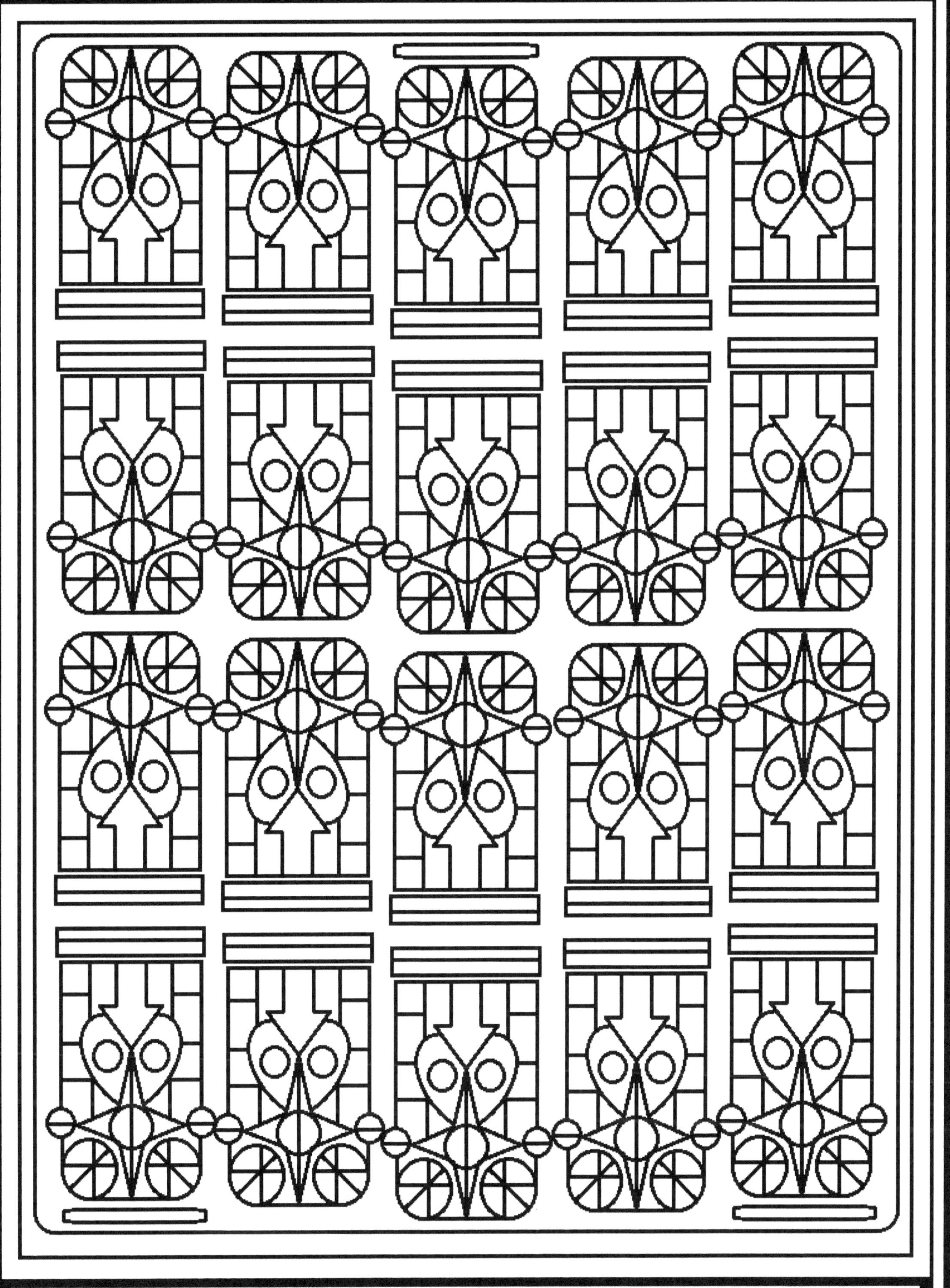

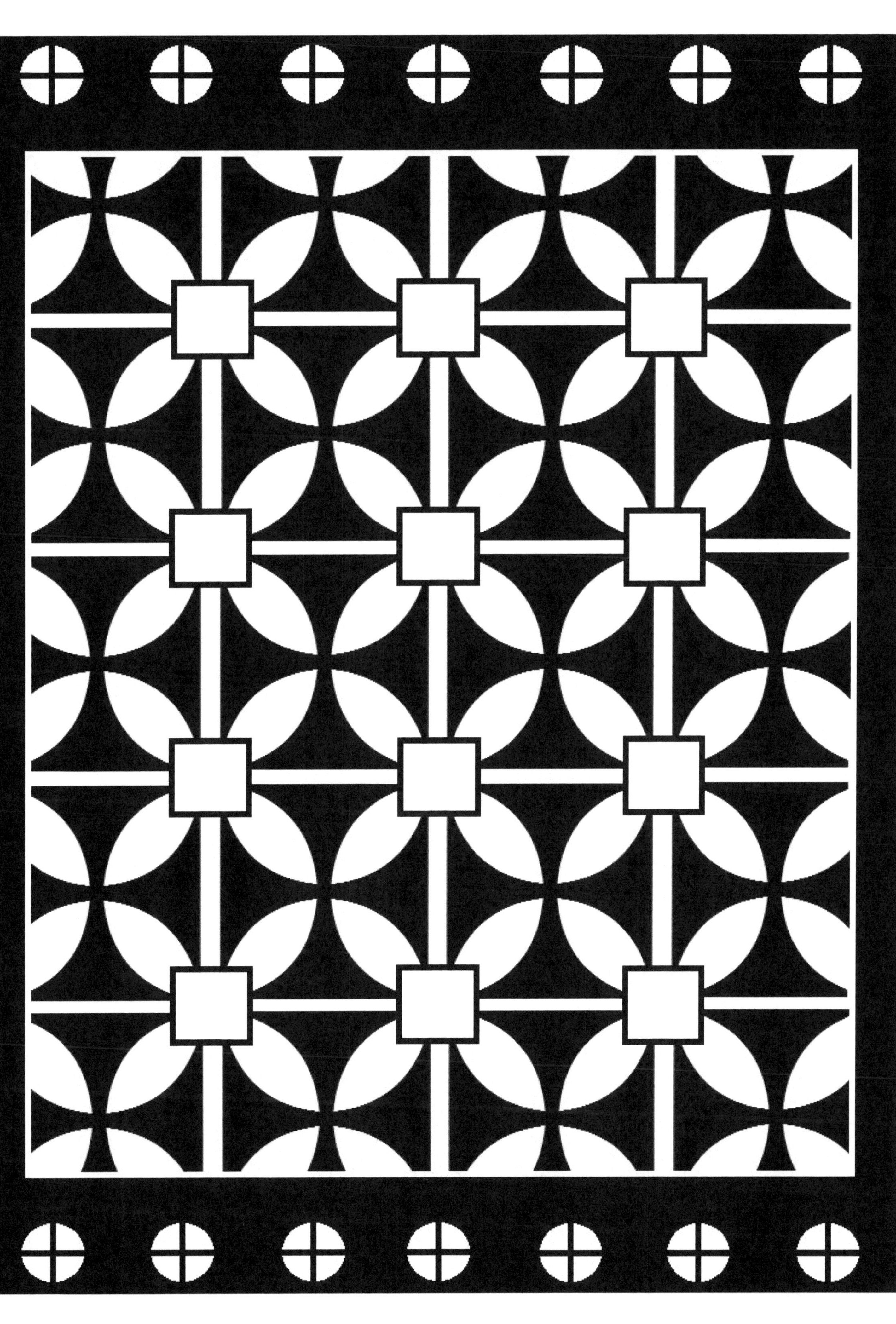

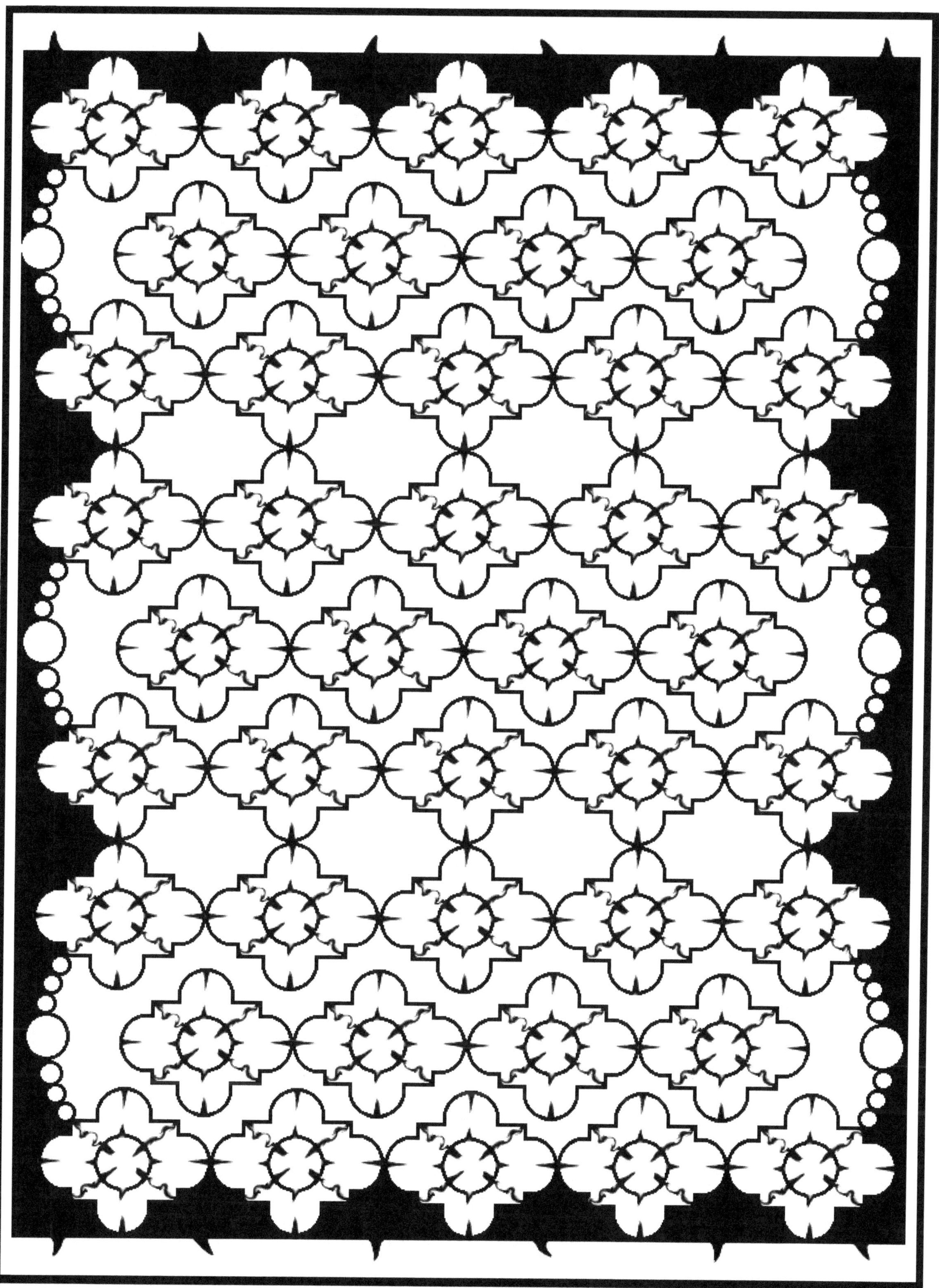

Bella Blue
Adult Coloring Book

find it on Amazon.com

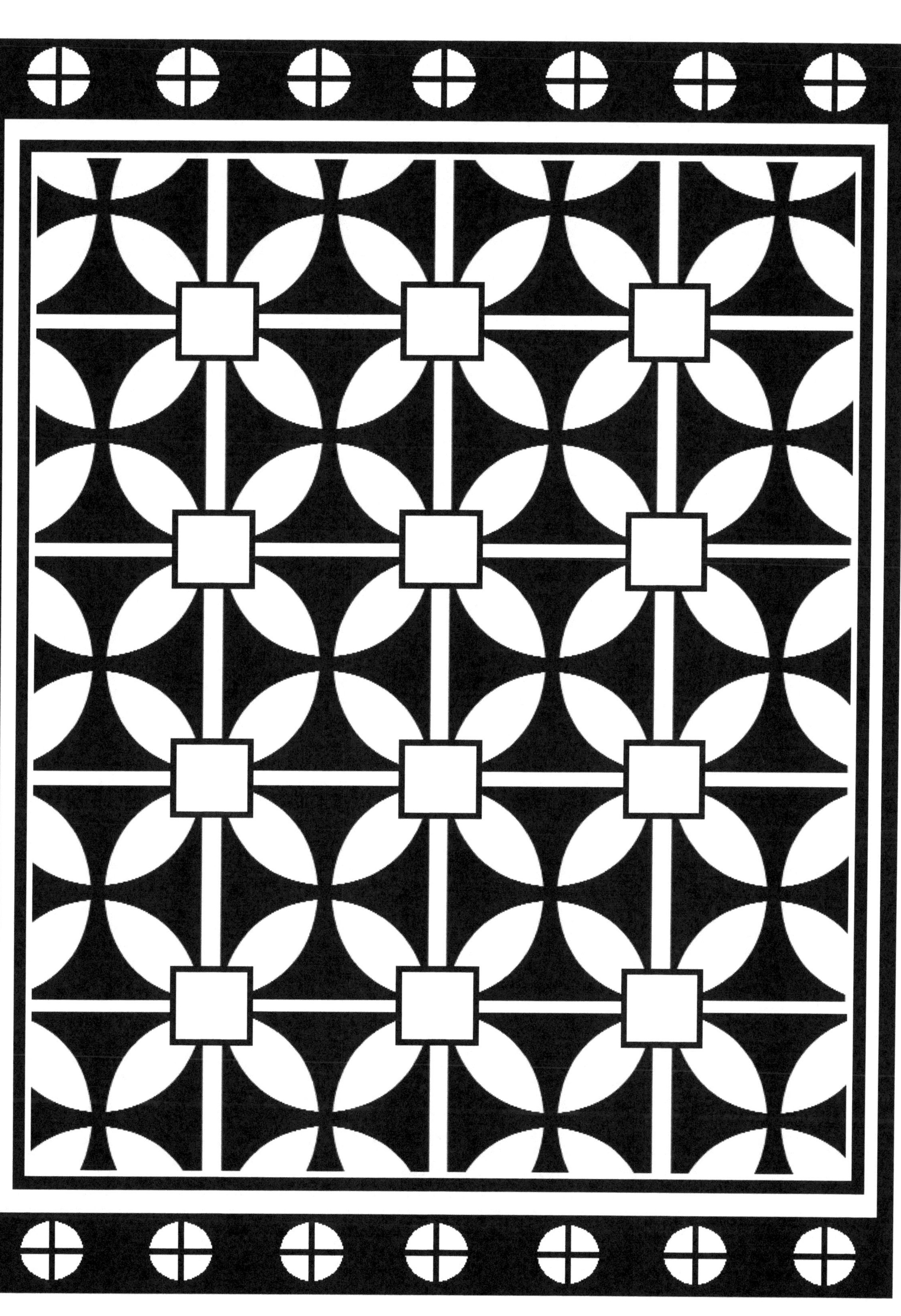

Bella Blue
Adult Coloring Book

find it on Amazon.com

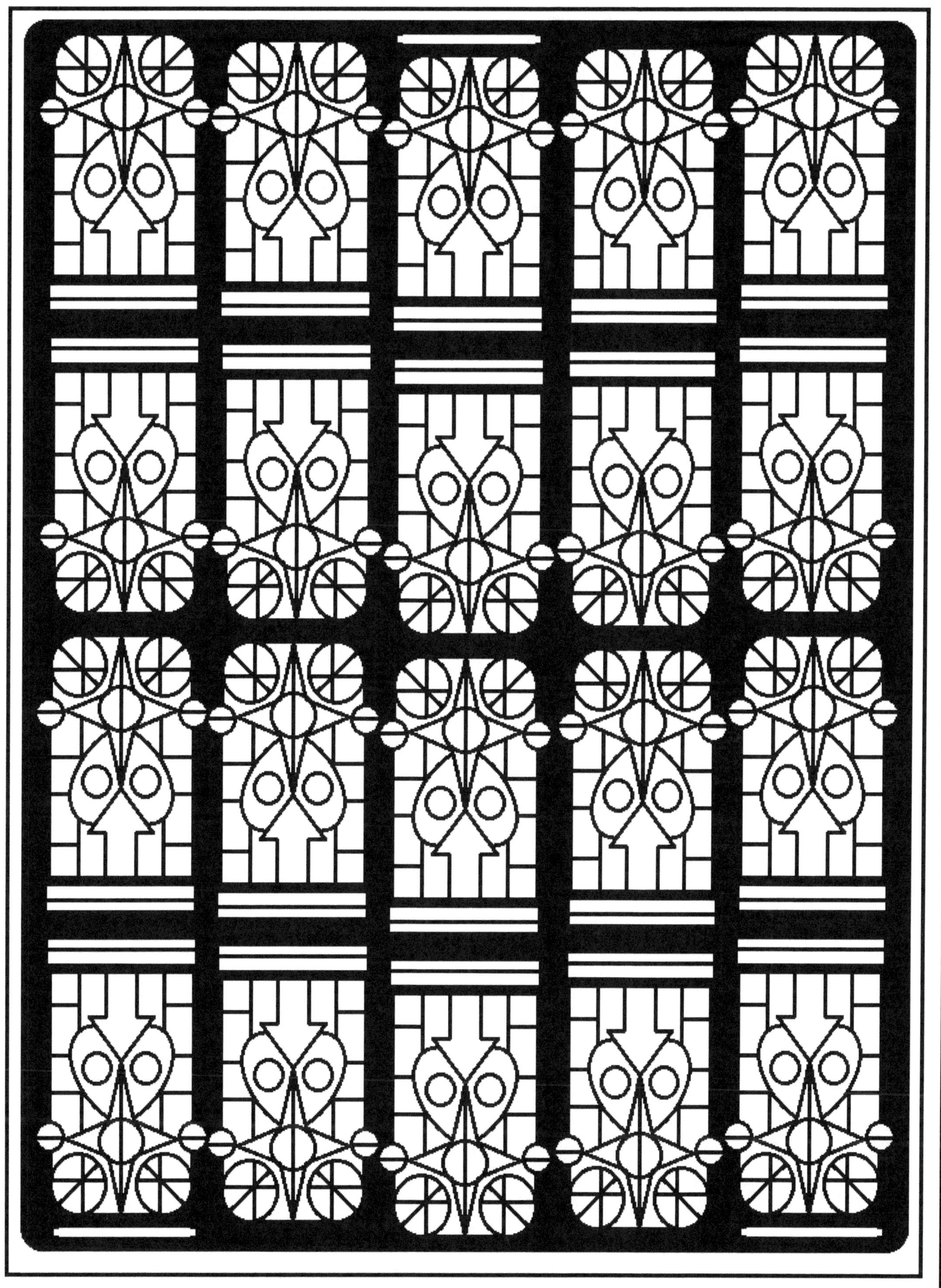

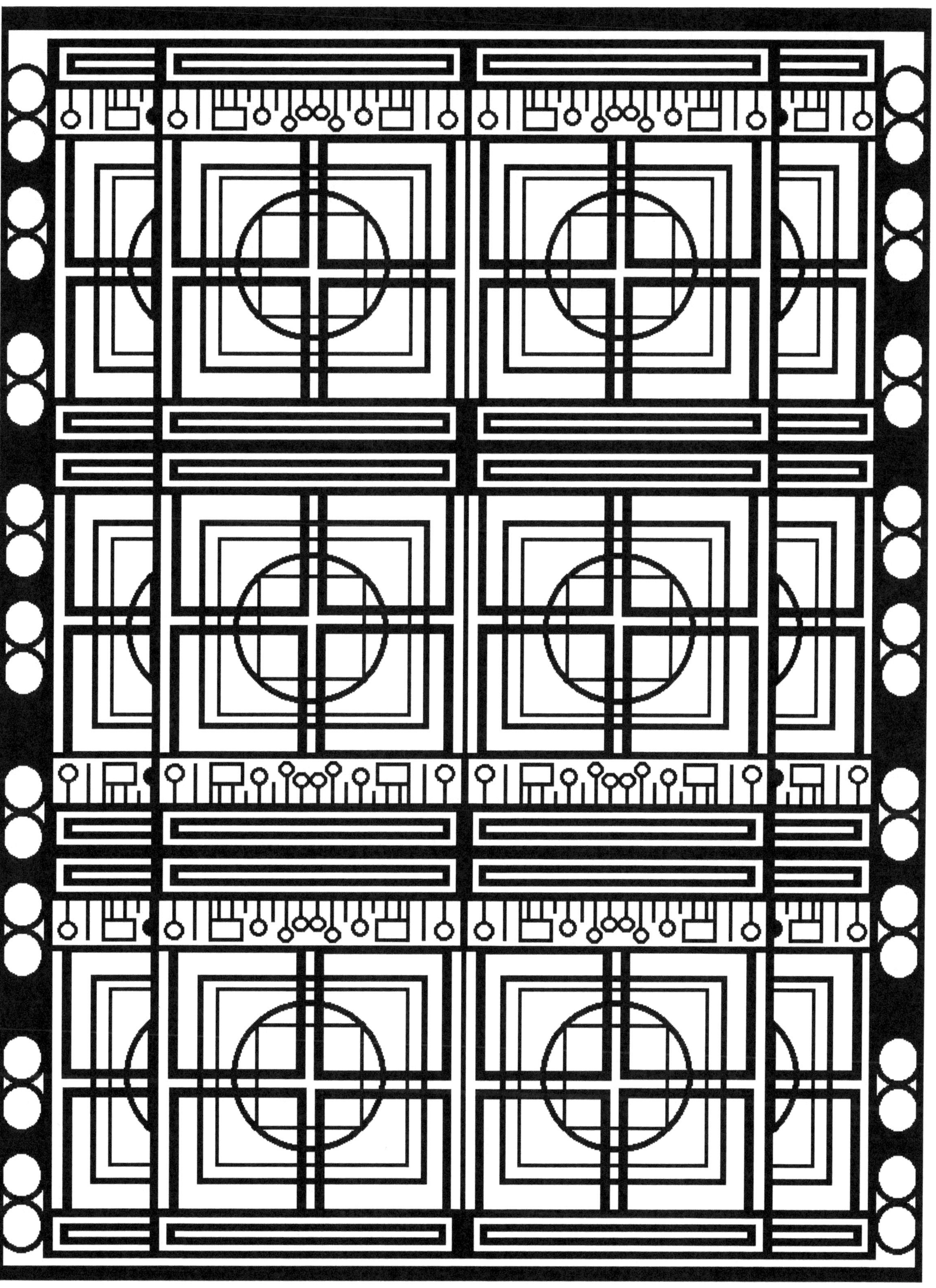

Bella Blue
Adult Coloring Book

find it on Amazon.com

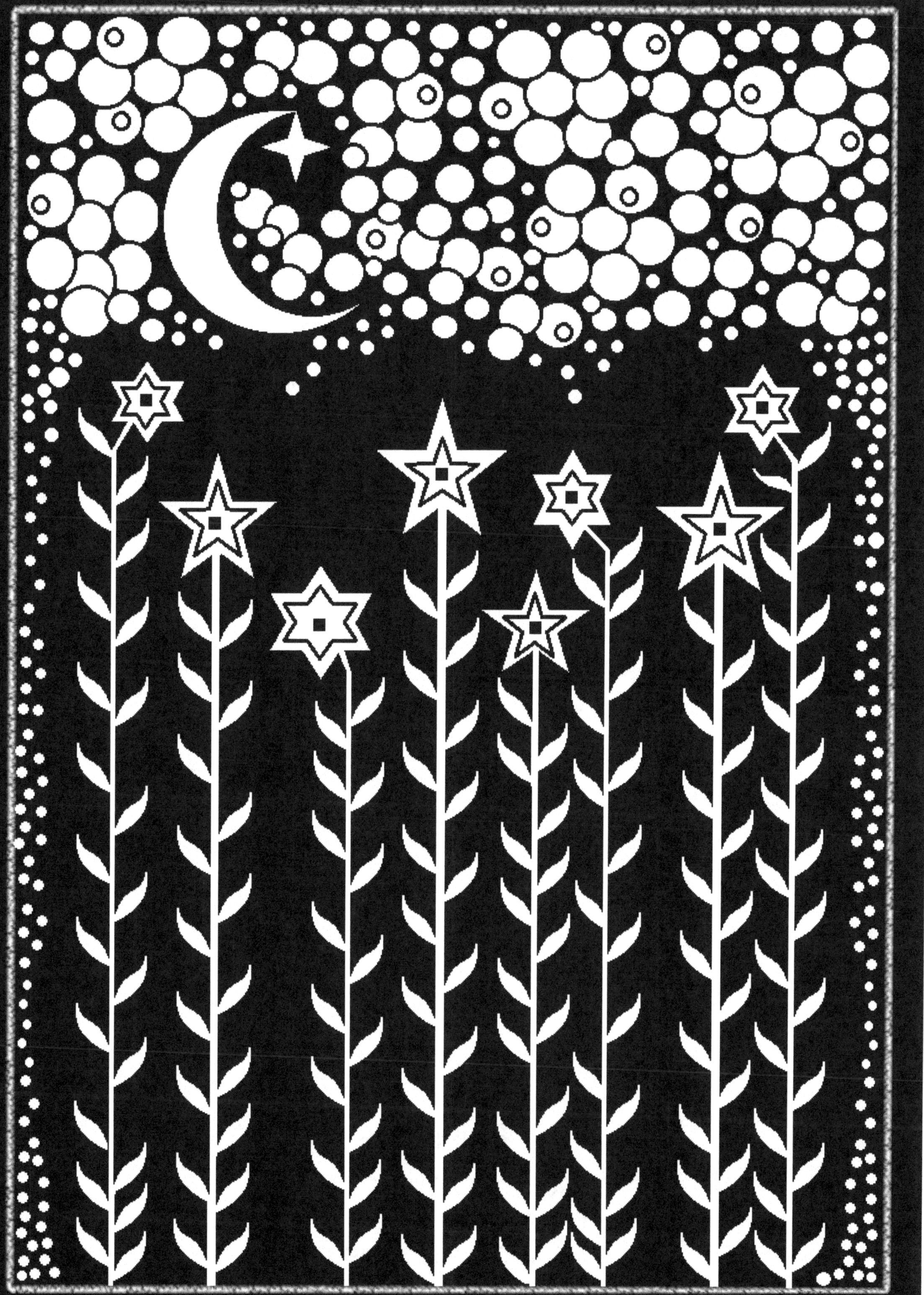

Bella Blue
Adult Coloring Book

find it on Amazon.com

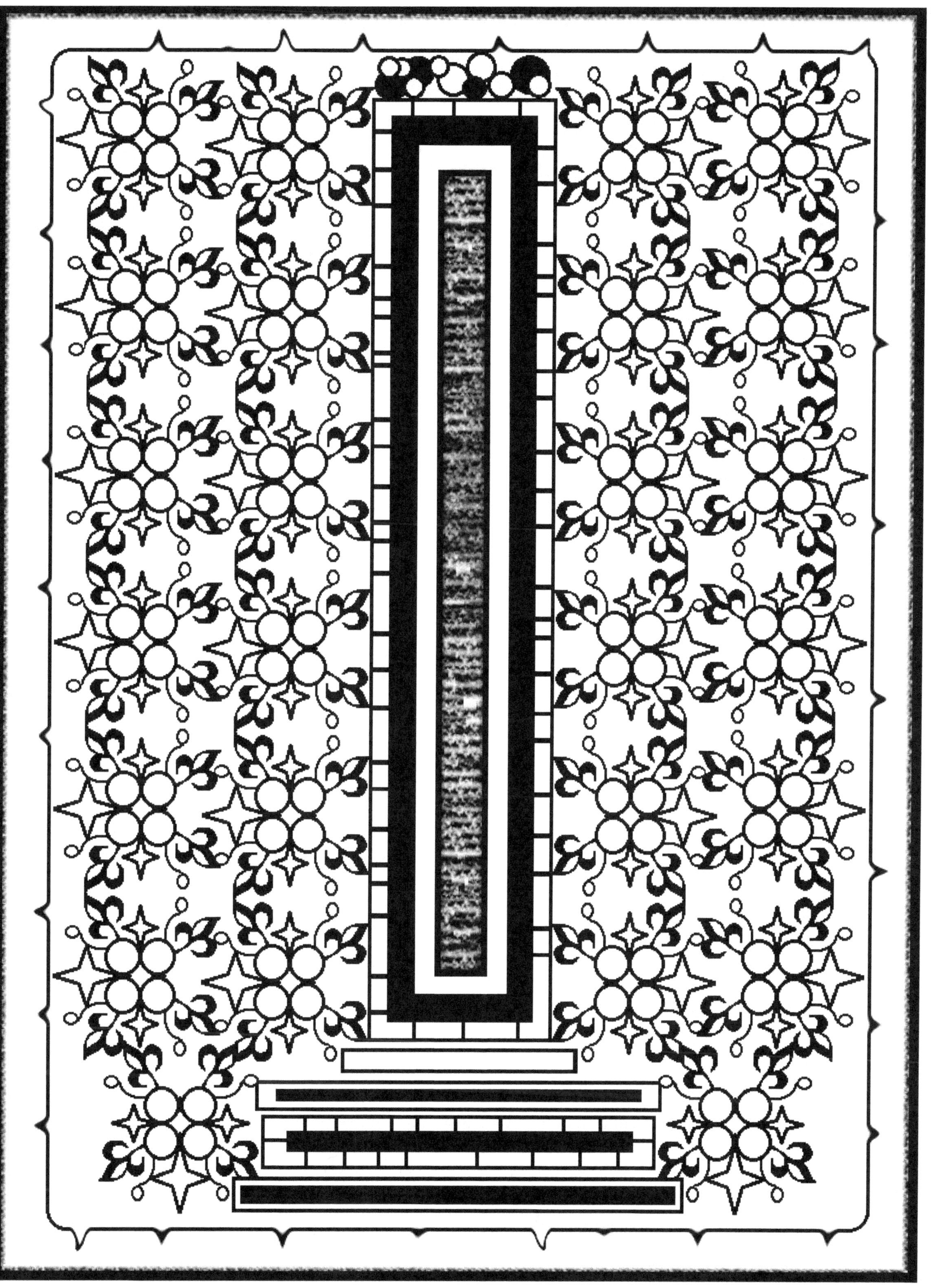

Bella Blue
Adult Coloring Book

find it on Amazon.com

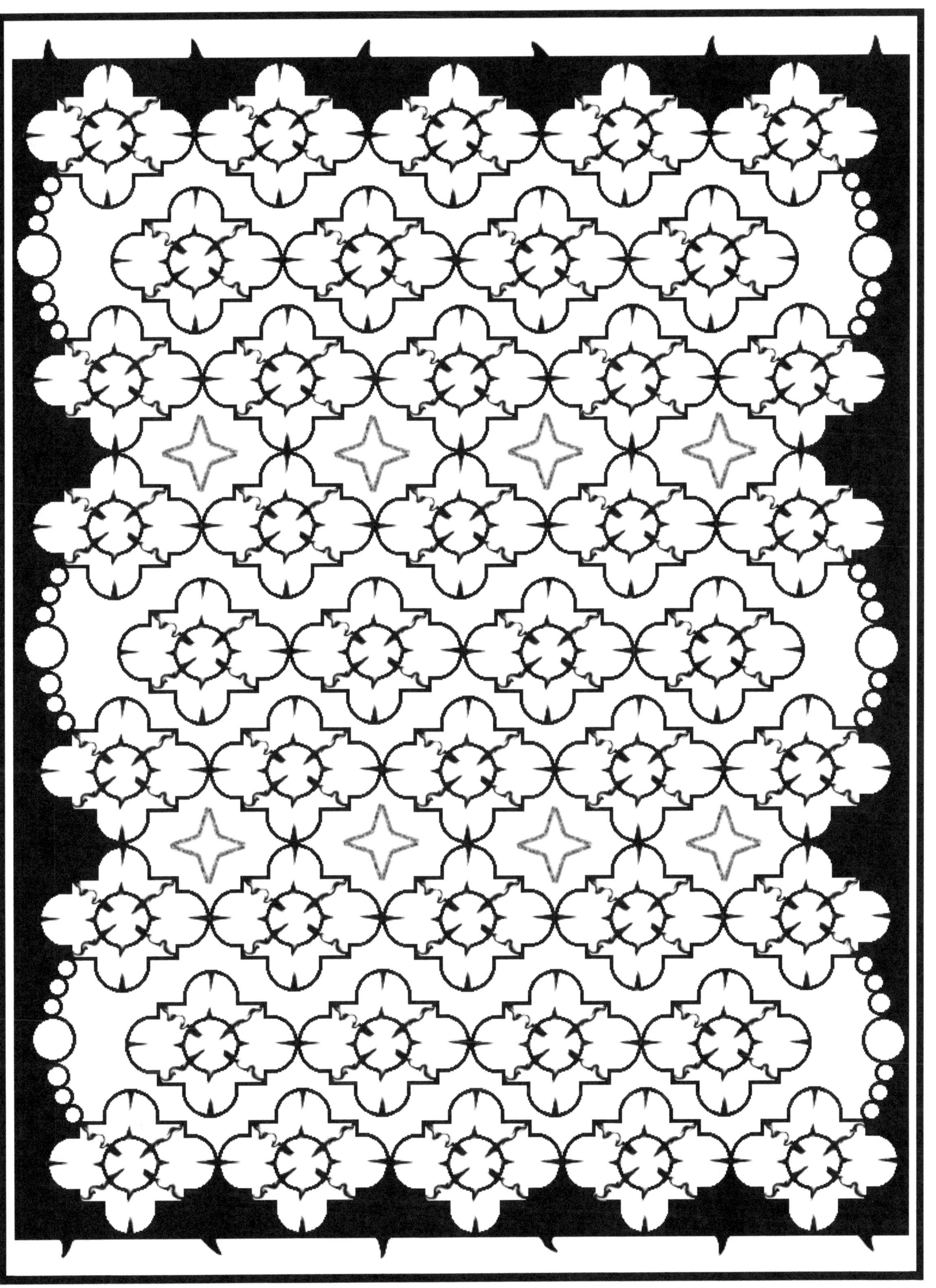

Bella Blue
Adult Coloring Book

find it on Amazon.com

www.ingramcontent.com/pod-product-compliance
Lightning Source LLC
LaVergne TN
LVHW061249100826
845148LV00008B/1067
* 9 7 8 0 9 7 9 4 6 0 9 1 3 *